Living
Perfect Love

Self-Empowerment Rituals for Women

Foreword by: LOUISE L. HAY

Author: ANGELO A. ZAFFUTO, Ph.D.

Humantics MultiMedia Publishing
6965 El Camino Real
P.O. Box 105-105
Rancho La Costa, California 92009

LIVING PERFECT LOVE

Self-Empowerment Rituals for Women

Humantics MultiMedia Publishers
6965 El Camino Real, #105-105
Carlsbad, CA 92009, United States of America

Library of Congress Catalog Card Number: 96-94513
International Standard Book Number (ISBN): 0-9652851-0-3
Zaffuto Angelo A, Ph.D.
LIVING PERFECT LOVE
Self-Empowerment Rituals for Women
Bibliography:
Includes index.
1. Authorship and Illustrations: Zaffuto, Angelo A.

Dedication

To my mother Providenzia, a Sicilian immigrant,
who was the first woman in my life to enlighten me to the
importance of a woman's self-empowerment. She taught me the essence of
living perfect love and living harmoniously with all womankind. To my
twin brother, John Peter, who through all these years, has faithfully been a
supporter and reminder of mother's example.

Acknowledgements

Thank You All, for Sharing Your *Perfect Love* Energy
with
LIVING PERFECT LOVE,
Self-Empowerment Rituals for Women

I extend my first thanks to my dearest and gracious friend, Louise Hay, who has always proclaimed the truth of *"living perfect love"* in all her writings. I so appreciate her loving contributions and for suggesting this model title, *"living perfect love."*

To Ag'nike (Angel) the village Medicine Woman, of the Rio Agua Clara village, in South America. She was my mentor, and friend and opened my spiritual conscious awareness to *perfect love* energy. I thank her for the many loving days as my guide, taking me by the hand on the path of living *perfect love*. Also, to all of the other Rio Agua Clara native women for their example of daily living *perfect love* energy. To Piedad, my loyal and faithful friend and interpreter, who carefully and accurately clarified the *perfect love* energy of Ag'nike.

To Mike Bono of Santa Barbara, California, a long time personal friend, for his support and encouragement to take the challenge of writing on this subject and self-publishing. For his "instinctive advising," which he acquired from his beautiful mother, who daily lived in her *perfect love* energy. For Mike's many hours of laboring: designing, typesetting, proofing, and literally putting this book together.

To Ilena Rosenthal, Chairwoman and Director of the Board of the Humantics Foundation for Women, a very special friend who I dearly love. For contributing her beautiful soft, feminine energy, and advising me from a woman's point of view. For the many tireless hours of editing and rewriting which she so graciously and unselfishly provided for living *perfect love* energy.

To Alice Zaffuto, my faithful friend and sister in-law, who has through the years, believed in me and supported all of my endeavors.

To Marty Brastow, for her many hours of *perfect love* energy proof reading and sharing valuable suggestions to the manuscript. To Carol Blaut for her wonderful and kind female point of view and *perfect love* editing suggestions.

To the many, many wonderful and loving female friends and all my family members for their encouragement, and especially for their belief, that all women and men should be treated equally with *perfect love*. To all my female students, clients and friends who have so willingly trusted me with their problems over the years, and for opening my awareness and empathy toward the very nature of the feminine spirit. Without them, this book could not have been possible.

And finally, to Patty Ozios Zaffuto, my lovely former wife, who manifested her *perfect love* and bravely joined me on this incredible adventure. I am forever indebted to her safe keeping of the exquisite statue on the cover—symbol of *perfect love*.

With Much Gratitude and Love Always,

Angelo

LIVING PERFECT LOVE
Self-Empowerment Rituals
for Women

Table Of Contents

Dr. Zaffuto tells of his journey to the Colombian jungle to find his fortune dredging for gold. Instead, he meets Ag'nike, a native Medicine Woman, whose people practice self-empowerment meditation rituals for peace and happiness. Dr. Zaffuto is invited to these rituals and his own life is transformed.

Illustrations

"I AM"

The Essence of Perfect Love Energy

"*Perfect love* energy is the vibrational energy that brings harmony and balance to the human body and earthly life. Whenever you are consciously aware of your own *perfect love* energy, you experience that all good changes that will come, will come from the essence of your *perfect love* energy. We all possess this *perfect love* energy — abundantly, equally, and infinitely. It is the common bond and connection with all that exists in the Universe. In order to restore balance and harmony on earth, all humans will learn once again how to manifest and enjoy the empowerment of *perfect love* energy."

Received by Angelo Zaffuto, Ph.D., in 1981 from Ag'nike,
Medicine Woman of the Rio Agua Clara village, Colombia, South America

Foreword

by Louise L. Hay

I have known Dr. Angelo Zaffuto for some time. When we first met, he showed me a charred but intact, early copy of my book, *You Can Heal Your Life*. It was one of the few things that survived a fire that burned his house to the ground. We were instant friends.

Love is the most powerful healing force there is. We are only just beginning to understand the magnitude of the power of love. Learning to live a life of *perfect love* is the goal of all spiritually-minded people.

In Dr. Zaffuto's book, *Living Perfect Love, Self-empowerment Rituals for Women,* we are led to explore a pathway to this goal again. Being well in touch with the feminine spirit in his soul, Angelo has been a champion of women's issues for many years. His innate ability to listen and deeply understand women has been augmented professionally by his years as a sociologist and counselor. His self-empowerment courses and workshops for women have changed countless lives. *Living perfect love* is a way of empowering every aspect of our lives. Never has the world been more acutely aware of the vast numbers of women who endure abusive relationships because they feel powerless within themselves. I, like many of you, have been there too.

As we now approach the new millennium — potent change is inevitable. Women of all ages can and will take back their birthright of self-love, self-respect and abundance. Dr. Zaffuto's excellent Self-Empowerment Rituals for Women, when embraced and practiced regularly, will enable women to attract the love, health, and success we all deserve.

I recommend accompanying him in his journey to the deep jungle of South America as he meets and then embraces the teachings of a native Medicine Woman whose tribe lives in harmony and balance. Follow his lead as he shares with you the ancient wisdom of recognizing, creating, practicing, and living in *perfect love* energy. Join Angelo and me in knowing: *This moment is a new point of beginning for me right here and now. All is well in my world.*

Love Heals!

Louise L. Hay
May, 1996

International author and lecturer Louise L. Hay, is known for her best selling books, workshops and audiotapes on mind-body healing.

Introduction

Too many of us seem to believe that we are powerless to change the circumstances of our lives. I, however, cannot bring myself to believe this. As I have continued through the years to study and collect new information to improve on my first published work, *Alphagenics: How to Use Your Brain Waves to Improve Your Life,* I have come to the conclusion that there is a natural and lasting philosophy of keeping mind and body in harmony and balance. The product of my research and life experience in the wake of *Alphagenics* is *Living Perfect Love: Self-Empowerment Rituals for Women.*

My inspiration for writing this book comes from three very important people. The first woman in my life was, of course, my mother, Providenzia a natural born Sicilian who daily practiced her own ritual of self-empowerment which helped her to live in *perfect love.* The second person was my father, a Sicilian immigrant who taught me the ways to respect and appreciate my mother's independence and ability to raise three boys in harmony and balance. I remember my Papa saying to me, "It would be a better world my son if all women could freely express their 'independenzia' ... and you shoulda some'a day find a wife like'a you mama."

The third person was a woman who brought my past and present into harmony and focus for me. Ag'nike (Ag-NEEK-eh), Medicine Woman of the Rio Agua Clara natives, who live on the banks of a river deep in the heart of the Colombian jungle. She helped me realize I was a Medicine Man for my own people. True, I held a Ph.D. in Sociology from Saint Andrews University in London and had spent many years counseling female clients, conducting Self-Mastery workshops and running clinics in Los Angeles and Santa Barbara, California. All of this might indeed qualify me to be a kind of Medicine Man, but I felt unworthy to be included in Ag'nike's league. Why? I had no knowledge of the supreme medicine she was destined to teach me, although intuitively I knew I had made my trip into the jungle to learn from her.

I now believe Ag'nike was a messenger sent to transform the entirety of my vision in what was possibly the most self-centered phase of my life. Seeking adventure, I had come to South America to dredge its rich rivers for gold. I had penetrated deep into the jungle to check the status of my gold-dredging claims. (A "claim" was the section of land (or river) allotted to whosoever was willing to set up stakes, mine or dredge it, and then turn the resources over to the Colombian government in exchange for money.) In Colombia at that time, the claims were free. I was ecstatic. I would take from the earth and grow rich.

I learned instead, that as we take, we must give back. Mother Earth gives us food, materials for shelter, and even — as the river did for me — the very ideas that allow us to prosper. I was *claiming, taking, getting* — and about to make off with it all. Had I done so, I would have been a bandit. Yet the presence of Ag'nike in my life changed everything. She showed me, in her compassionate, wise way, that I was a part of a vast continuum of universal energy. I had my small but distinct place in the balance of it all.

We do not exist in a vacuum, nor do we exist as the center of our own universe. We are part of an exquisite whole that connects us all. As Ag'nike walked me through the jungle, I learned that the bond that ties everything to everything else is the energy of the universe. It is this universal energy that gives us everything we need through its *perfect love*. I learned from Ag'nike, that even objects I had thought to be inanimate have this *perfect love* — the fragile beauty of a plant in bloom, the colors in a rainbow, the water of the river reflecting the sky. The effect these treasures have on us is the energy of *perfect love*, explained Ag'nike. It is solidifying and empowering. And recognizing this connection and empowerment is the key to a happier existence.

The rituals Ag'nike and her people in Colombia shared with me are the rituals I have modified to create the "path" into Alpha that you will be shown in this book. Alpha is a state of mental consciousness that opens our higher spiritual levels of creating and learning, from which we can access a wealth of new ideas, knowledge and wisdom, including — in Ag'nike's magical words — "seeing the unseen and hearing the unheard."

I have found in my counseling that the path to Alpha is the gateway to our realm of self-transformation. We are able to program our minds when we are very centered, very relaxed — feeling and acknowledging that the *perfect love* energy in the universe exists to empower us and others to overcome our insecurities and fears. *The path to Alpha* opens our consciousness to the information we need to change our attitudes, behavior and general orientation to our daily life. We are all our own worst enemy, and it has never been easy to find a way into that adversary's head to turn off the spigot of constant discontent and disapproval.

Ag'nike's self-empowerment Alpha rituals can be applied to any kind of self-improvement, and as long as you continue to practice them, their results are limitless. I encourage you to carefully read Part One and Part Two of this book and become completely comfortable with the principles of Alpha self-transformation before you tackle the specific issues you wish to change about yourself. Part One explains the Rio Agua Clara native women's societal structure and the way they interpret and apply *perfect love* in their meditations and daily life. The self-empowerment rituals taught in this book are derived from the Rio Agua Clara natives' fireside and waterfall rituals, and it is important that you understand the workings of their "path" before you experiment with your own. Part Two of this book explores the concept of *perfect love* energy and the dynamics it offers us for self-transformation. Part Three contains step-by-step meditation rituals for a variety of self-improvement arenas and issues. You will benefit best from Part Three after you familiarize yourself first with Parts One and Two.

It is my hope that all of my readers will find the philosophy of Ag'nike's living *perfect love* accessible enough to weave into their daily existence. Working with women in therapy, I have found that it is self-love and self-empowerment that confer happiness, confidence and, inevitably, the positive changes all of us seek. As the world we live in continues to produce chaotic currents of imbalance and the need to be free from abusive relationships and disharmony, our ability to find peace, tranquility and order for ourselves is essential. *The self-empowered woman creates this from within herself. She has no need to look elsewhere. She has everything she needs.*

As you practice your *perfect love* rituals, you will find that your spiritual, psychological and physiological balance is no longer determined by outside uncertainties. You have dominion over your entire being. You have all the necessary tools to explore the limitless potentials of your spirit, mind and body. You are the master of your spirit, mind and body — and you will discover that the path to doing so is enjoyable, easy and completely within your reach.
Enjoy the Journey!

Angelo A. Zaffuto, Ph.D., Rancho La Costa, California

Part One

South American Native Women Teach
Perfect Love Energy
and
Self-Empowerment Rituals

"I AM"

Self-Empowered
to Utilize the Limitless
Potentials of
My Spirit, Mind and Body.

CHAPTER 1

Ag'nike, Our Teacher of Perfect Love

In May 1981, my partner Ken and I arrived at the Rio Agua Clara village deep in the Colombian jungle. We had ventured into mining for gold and had traveled to a remote part of the jungle to take a look at our gold-dredging claims. Ken had arranged with the Colombian ministry of mines for us to claim and dredge several thousand acres of riverbed. He had owned and operated a gold-dredging company in Colombia for some 17 years. He had offered me a share of his company a few months before, and I accepted enthusiastically. Gold! I couldn't wait to see it for myself.

This was the beginning of an adventure that would never end.

I met Ken in Cali as soon as I could arrange to leave the United States. He explained that people couldn't just rush off into the jungle unprepared — we had to get provisions together and plan such a trip carefully. Ken had already spent several months in the Rio Agua Clara region, searching out the potential for gold. He even made a friend of Omar, a local tribal native

Fifteen years have passed and Ag'nike's magical words compel me to write about her *perfect love* energy—the essence of her self-empowerment.

who knew the river well and helped Ken to choose and work his claims. Excited all the more by the prospect of the jungle, the adventure and unknown, I talked Ken into leaving as soon as we could.

The Rio Agua Clara originates high in the Andes and empties into the Pacific Ocean. A quiet, gentle river most of the year, upon our arrival it was swollen and moving swiftly because of recent heavy rains. Motoring and occasionally paddling upriver from the little town of Buena Ventura, we found ourselves challenged by the current and rapids in our heavy dugout canoes. It took us several hours to reach the meeting point we had arranged with Omar by way of a message that had been traveling to him by word of mouth for several days. He met us on the bank of the river, smiling and waving. Weary by now, we were grateful for his skill with the canoes and happily turned the navigation over to him.

The river shared its perfect love energy, providing the way into the thick jungle.

Angelo entering the village with two young native guides.

Omar's small village was tucked into the shade of thickly growing hardwood trees on the banks of the Rio Agua Clara. It had taken us nine hours of canoeing through the thick jungle to arrive. As we climbed from our cumbrous dugouts, I observed a cluster of some dozen large grass huts perched above the ground on stilts. Native women in bright but scanty cotton garments were washing clothes and minding children who were playing all about. Ken and Omar led me into the center of the village and introduced me to the chief and two of his three wives. The villagers evidently knew Ken and were excited to see both

I was uneasy as I entered the village.

of us. I was immediately struck by their exuberant warmth and hospitality they had already marked a site for us on the other side of the river and graciously helped us get settled. Gratefully accepting their warm welcome and kindness, I had little idea of what was in store for me. I did not yet know my life would never be the same.

Women as Leaders

For the first few days, Ken supervised the bringing in of supplies and equipment and the preparation of our campsite to begin dredging for gold. Like Ken, the natives had been working the dredging business for years, and I was the only one who was a novice. Feeling a little misplaced and awkward, I did the best I could to smile and be friendly, mingle with the natives and pass the time.

I found that I could relax almost immediately. The native women were more open and generous than I ever could have

Ag'nike's village, with gold dredging in the foreground.

been in their place. Because many of the men were away from the village at dredging sites the majority of the time, the women managed most of the village affairs. They supervised the construction of huts, educated the children, and prepared the natural, nutritious meals. Though the huts were large, I learned that life for these natives was nomadic. Their primary livelihood came from diving for gold nuggets, and they would pick up and move whenever necessary.

It was mostly the men who dredged — either working for mining companies or independently. Some of the men, however, had the job of providing food (mostly by fishing, sometimes by hunting) and protecting the village as needed. I soon realized, that the women were completely in charge. As a sociologist, I found this remarkable and fascinating. The men would seek the women's advice, and even though the village chief was male, (this was apparently necessary for the village to participate in outer-tribal council meetings) his three wives commanded and advised him on all matters. I learned that it was common for the village men to have more than one wife. There were so many more women than men that the women had decided it was proper to share!

I was reminded of my home life with Mama. My mother truly managed our family with her perfect love energy.

The Rio Agua Clara natives enjoyed an unusual and amicable balance of power and roles and seemed pleased and content to live this way. There were no weapons, not even spears for hunting (the natives used lassos) — and no lawmakers or police. The villagers had no doors to lock, and showed no fear of one another or for the white people who made contact with them for the business of gold. I wondered why?

The Fire Dance Ritual

One morning, Ken asked me if I would like to meet the village "doctor" or Medicine Woman. Her name was Ag'nike (Ag-NEEK-eh), or "angel," in the native tongue. I was mildly curious and thought it would be interesting to see what she looked like, at the very least.

We walked toward a hut that was different from the others. On either side of the front entrance, there were two statues carved from soft, palm tree trunks. The statue on the right was of a man raising a staff to the heavens, and on the left was a statue of a woman nursing her baby. I learned later that the statue with the man holding the staff symbolized our connection to the energy of the universe, and the statue of the mother nursing her baby celebrated newborn infants bringing *perfect love* energy to us at their birth. Ag'nike saw us coming and greeted us warmly at the entrance to her hut. To my surprise, she was not the old, bent woman I had imagined, but stood straight like a girl, petite and smiling, wearing a simple cotton dress. I guessed she must be in her thirties.

"JolÖ (hello)," said Ken. With his rudimentary knowledge of the native language, he expressed to her as best he could, that I was a doctor and friend of his who, like Ag'nike herself, was a healer of body and mind. He left us together to get acquainted with the help of Piedad (Pee-eh-DAHD), a medical worker with the mining company who had become my tireless interpreter.

Ag'nike, true to the spirit the natives had shown us, took me under her wing. She invited me the next day to attend the ritual of the fire dance. All the villagers sat in a circle around a large fire — much like the campfires I used to make on the beaches of Santa Barbara. The children clustered in front of the women and the men grouped themselves on the opposite side.

Statue of a mother nursing her baby—symbol of *perfect love.*

Ken, Piedad (though she was a woman) and I had been brought to the men's side and were sitting next to Ag'nike. No one said a word. I began to wonder what we were going to do. Ag'nike caught me glancing around and leaned over to speak. Piedad translated in a whisper, "She says to look into the flames. As you look, the flame will speak to you and show you the path to harmony and balance." Ag'nike nodded and spoke again. "Sit and remain quiet," Piedad continued. "Look into the fire for the unseen. See how the flames are continually changing. It is a magic dance. You must look carefully, and also hear the unheard sounds. You must listen to the music of the flames. It is always perfectly changing."

When the ritual was over, Ag'nike asked me how I felt. I thought for a moment and then replied that I wasn't sure. I looked around at the rest of the natives. They all appeared very happy and content as they talked and smiled and laughed, the children running around playing with each other. I turned to Ag'nike. "I feel the way everyone here is feeling," I explained. "I am celebrating this wonderful moment being at peace and feeling contentment. To be here with you is a special gift and an experience beyond all my expectations."

I gave Piedad time to translate properly, as I wanted to make sure Ag'nike got every word of what I said.

As I waited for Piedad, I became aware of the strange and powerful high I was feeling — a consciousness high that brought me an immense sensation of love, beauty and warm energy. *Wow,* I thought to myself. I couldn't believe that only a week ago I was thousands of miles away in my office in Santa Barbara counseling unhappy, troubled people. What a contrast! As I

While looking down the river, I couldn't believe that only a week ago I was in Santa Barbara

sat in the company of these natives in harmony and balance. I felt the essence of *perfect love* energy that had definitely been missing from my office. I wanted nothing more than for all of my friends, family and clients to be here sharing this wonderful force that I could acknowledge only as *love*.

The realization dawned on me that from the very first moment when I arrived in the village, the natives all seemed to be consistently manifesting a state of ongoing contentment — even joy. I wondered what was the source. The fireside ritual? Was it a special event or a holiday?

The Essence of Perfect Love

I had apparently not arrived at any kind of special time. The three days I had spent in the village had been three ordinary days. As the villagers dispersed, I motioned to Piedad to follow me. "We're going to Ag'nike's hut," I said. "I have many questions I want to ask." Ag'nike received us graciously, as I knew she would. She led us behind the hut to where a beautiful stream trickled, surrounded by lush and exotic plants. It was a natural sanctuary. She motioned for us to sit on the ground next to the stream. She sat down beside us and we all concentrated on the moving

Black tribe people visiting Ag'nike.

waters. Anxious to get started, I broke the silence. "Ag'nike," I asked, "why are the villagers always so cheerful and happy?"

Ag'nike turned to me slowly. "Because it is so," she replied. "It is the measure of our behavior here. In our village, we endure as one people. We aspire to live in the energy *of perfect love.*"

"How do you stay in this state?" I inquired.

Ag'nike taught me to celebrate the everlasting presence of God's *perfect love* energy.

"We manifest our *perfect love energy* every day so that we may live in harmony and enjoy good health," she answered. "Everyone is taught from childhood that it is better to live in *perfect love* and feel happy than to live without *perfect love* and lament and feel sick."

Ag'nike explained that *perfect love energy* could only be experienced by individual acknowledgment of its presence. "You know it is present when you are feeling genuinely wonderful, in harmony with all life and free of all anxiety. It transmits a sacred energy that makes you confident, in much the same way as when you have successfully completed a task and your spirit is lifted high. Anything you do will be affected by your *perfect love* energy — if you choose to recognize it and use it." She paused. "It is food for the spirit, as necessary as food for the body. Our people cannot live without it."

I sat quietly, listening, taking in her spiritual and magical words "Perfect love empowers you. Everything, every person with whom you come in contact will recognize and reflect your empowerment." She gestured toward the center of the village, "Creatures," she ran her fingers through the earth of the jungle floor. "will perceive your kindness and feel safe in your presence. All plant life will blossom for you to adore its natural and beautiful energy and to honor you with its fragrance." She pointed to a

"The little children shall recognize your empowerment."

wild ginger plant just coming into bloom. "As you look into the sky," (we followed her arm as it swept toward the sky), "the sun shares its energy and is there to provide loving warmth and light to guide you through the day as a faithful companion. Most of all, you will feel loved by all around you." She stood up and reached with both her arms to the celestial sky. "All that is in the universe exhibits and esteems *perfect love* energy." She dropped her arms. "That is our first lesson."

As Ag'nike spoke her magical words, she appeared to be connected to all.

I sat quietly after Piedad translated. Ag'nike began to walk around. "Our second lesson is that when we do not honor and experience *perfect love*, we feel out of control, like a river after a monsoon rain — creating turmoil, devastation, uprooting vegetation and finally total chaos. Ignoring *perfect love*, our whole life is affected — we live in fear feeling *powerless*, out of balance and eventually become ill and die."

I thought of the many people I knew in California who lived with the imbalance Ag'nike described. She was so right. I shook my head, taking in the truth of her words. She noticed. "Come to our waterfall ritual," she invited, smiling, "you will learn more about how to unveil your own infinite *perfect love* energy."

The Waterfall Ritual

The following morning I was led by Ag'nike and some 40 women and children into the depths of the jungle, away from the village. As a special honor, I had been invited to the ritual usually reserved for women and children only.

Native women preparing for the hike to the waterfall.

I would be the only adult man present. I followed behind Ag'nike, flanked by Piedad. We came upon a clearing graced by a lovely waterfall and a crystal stream. Birds sang everywhere. I was in awe.

A semi-circle of rocks faced the waterfall. Ag'nike asked me to select a rock to sit on that connected with my energy. The others took seats on the remaining rocks. The ceremony began.

I learned from Piedad that all present were thanking the waterfall and stream for their celestial energy and presents that day. Then there was silence. Everyone sat on their rock and stared at the waterfall for what seemed to be a very long time. Then Ag'nike rose, and she motioned for us all to follow her as she led us through the jungle back to the village. Again, for the duration of the trek, no one said a word. Except for the sounds of our footsteps through the undergrowth, total transcending silence reigned.

> Mesmerized by the energy of the waterfall, I didn't realize that time stood still.

Back at the village, I turned to Ag'nike to ask my many questions. What had taken place for the 40 minutes or more we spent doing nothing at the waterfall? Ag'nike's reply was clear and simple.

"We partake of the ritual to reinforce our self-empowerment and remain in the spirit of perfect love. It is the one and only energy that upholds balance and harmony in our lives."

> God's Empowerment is manifested in Her *perfect love* energy—"You possess It."

"How?" I wanted to know. How did this silent ritual provide empowerment and love? "You must first learn, as you did at the fireside ritual, to see that which is not seen and hear that which is not heard," returned Ag'nike. "There are ever-changing learning experiences and discoveries for your empowerment."

The Powerful Energies

I learned from Ag'nike that there were many powerful energies — always new and always changing — in the waterfall and fireside rituals. When we open our awareness to these energies, they unite our higher consciousness with our own *perfect love*. This unity creates an unseen vibrational force that brings harmony and balance to our lives. If we keep our *perfect love* energy active, we experience peace and freedom from all fear.

"Any good change that will come will come from the essence of your perfect love energy," Ag'nike told me. "All that is, will house its own energy. This authority

Patty with Piedad, my interpreter, at the waterfall.

has always existed in the universe. We must invite and welcome this energy from all sources to us and unite it with our own *perfect love*. That is the purpose of the fireside and waterfall rituals. When we permit our *perfect love* energy to be revealed, we create harmony and gratification. When we do not, we manifest disharmony and fear. Believe me, it's quite simple."

I was made aware that all energy is one with God. And that the You in me, is the same as the You in You.

Unveiling Perfect Love

For the next seven days, I attended the fireside ritual and the waterfall ritual at every opportunity. One beautiful morning at the waterfall, Ag'nike gave me special attention. "Angelo," she called to me. "I would like very much for you to experience the revelation of your own *perfect love* energy this morning. As you begin to study the waterfall, give yourself the gift of *perfect love*. Look first at your reflection in the stream." She pointed at the water beneath us. "Identify your image, feel the water as it flows through your reflection. Think about the *perfect love* that dances in the water as it passes through the image of your face. Listen to the water. You will hear it say *I love Angelo.* Listen keenly. The sounds of the water will tell you that it is love. *I am love, I am love,* it will say. Repeat after it. I am love. Feel all the emotions of love. Be filled with it, let the feelings overcome you, allow the eyelids of your higher consciousness to open. Soon you will see the unseen, as you are hearing the unheard. *I am love.*"

I recalled Louise Hay saying in her book, *You Can Heal Your Life*, "Look at your reflection in the mirror and say 'I love you.'"

Angelo at Ag'nike's waterfall.

I sat down on my rock, preparing myself for the ritual. The others were waiting politely as Ag'nike gave her instruction. "Just like this waterfall," Ag'nike raised her arm, "we are constantly changing. When you return to the village, it will be a different village. All the people will be different. Since it is true that we are always actively changing, it is also true that our *perfect love* energy, if we are not inspired to keep it active, will be left behind as we drift away. The waterfall energy drifts downstream and leaves the earth behind, does it not? The flame of the fire goes up in smoke and leaves us behind. If we leave our *perfect love* behind, Angelo, pain and suffering will follow. Each time you come to this place, separate yourself from the mundane issues in your world and repeat *I am love* as I have told it to you. When you leave here, you will be a different person than when you came."

The ritual began. All turned their faces to the waterfall and silence reigned. As I stared into the tumbling water, trying to see what I was previously not able to see and hear what I could not previously hear, I remembered myself as a young boy in Rochester, New York. Walking in the fresh, white snow of our very cold winters, I would stare as hard as I could at the snowflakes dancing thickly in the air and landing on my upturned face.

Each of the flakes was unique, I had learned in school. I let myself become mesmerized, staring for the longest time. I felt peace, awe, the roaring sounds of silence and an overwhelming emotion which I did not recognize at the time was love. I felt exhilarated out there by myself — strong and powerful and confident. What a wonderful thing the snow was, I thought. I would run out into the snowflakes every time the sky grew gray and powdered them over the city. Sitting at the waterfall with the natives, I realized I had already developed a *perfect love* ritual of my own as a boy.

Many of us have already experienced a perfect love ritual of our own.

In the days to follow, Ag'nike and I spent many hours together comparing the different methods we used for healing and meditation. I explained to her the basics of Alphagenics, the mind-programming I had developed and taught in Santa Barbara. She understood everything. I realized, how-

Even the young children knew more about living *perfect love* than I did.

ever, that I had much more to learn from her ancient wisdom of *perfect love* energy.

Over the years, as I continued to counsel and make videotapes for self-improvement, I have come to believe that we in the Western world have left behind the healing power of simple, natural beauty that the Rio Agua Clara natives were able to put to work so effectively for themselves. By committing first to *perfect love* in front of their waterfall, the native women then withdrew from all external sensory awareness. They blocked distractions and, in psychological terms, displaced their egos from their bodies, minds and immediate environment. They were then able to focus *all* their energies on one thought alone. In so doing, they entered a passive aware state of concentration.

They allowed themselves to access a world of perception that is the key to self-transformation — a state in which the soul, fed by love, empowers the mind, the body and the spirit. Whether one calls this a religious, mystical or psychic experience is irrelevant. To me, it is an essential experience — one that is generally not attained by most Western women. The world of perception taught to me by Ag'nike was the same world I had entered through my exploration of Alpha, *but it was better*. It contained the ingredient of *perfect love* — which I had missed completely.

While at the waterfall, we heard the unheard, and saw the unseen.

Perfect love rituals have become a way of life for me since I met Ag'nike. Like most others, I face many daily challenges — health, relationships, paying bills, raising children, food, shelter, and on and on. *Perfect love* as the essence of my life philosophy has allowed me to feel and experience self-empowerment on a daily basis — as often as I practice the rituals I have created and modified for myself. Daily, I am able to manifest *perfect love* energy toward others and, in spite of all the challenges I continue to have, *I reap the benefit of living happily and feeling contented.*

Because most of us in the Western world are not lucky enough to have waterfalls coursing into our back-yards or fire rings that permit giant rustic fires, I have worked out an alternative to the mesmerizing natural rhythm of fire and water. I call it the "Alpha ritual path." It is the result of the brain wave research and training I conducted at the clinics and health centers I ran in California, integrated with the powerful principles

My most important lesson to learn was: "any good change that I will create, will come from my essence of *perfect love* energy."

Ag'nike shared with me. The original Alpha path, the basis of my writing and teaching called *Alphagenics*, has worked so effectively for those who used the *Alphagenics* program that I continue to teach this method for self-

As I looked back at Ag'nike's little hut, it was difficult to say good-bye.

35

transformation in my private counseling and work-shops today. *Perfect love* Alpha rituals are an integration of *Alphagenics* and the meditation rituals practiced by the native women of South America in a form that marries the modern with the ancient so that Western women in a male-dominated, hectic society can draw on their own, timeless, female power to become, as Ag'nike said, better and better every day.

Beneficial Effects of Your Alpha Rituals

- a marked increase in day-to-day courage
- an increased ability to cope
- greater strength and energy
- better health
- improved concentration
- accelerated learning
- ability to relax at will
- ability to control minor physical irritations
- harmony of mind, body and spirit
- Experience of self-empowerment
- increased self-worth
- increased self-love

Part Two

Self-Empowered
Women On the
Alpha Path

"I AM"

On the Path
of
Successful Living

CHAPTER

Preparing for the Self-Empowerment Alpha Path

Perfect love self-empowerment rituals will enable you to sense and put to use the positive energies already in your body and mind. By stilling your intellect and temporarily removing the self (known in psychology as the "ego") from your physical environment, you will be allowing yourself to rest in a mind state called "Alpha." With our mind in Alpha, we perceive much more of the non-physical world — what Ag'nike called "the unseen and the unheard." What we are really perceiving is our connection to all things around us, an energy connection that the process of growing up in our Western world has often obliterated.

Once you realize that your energy feeds into and feeds from all the energy in your environment in this beautiful, loving way, you will discover a wonderful awakening within you that brings a new, all-encompassing awareness. This awareness is the *essence* that *perfect love* rituals draw on to lead you to harmony of spirit, mind and body. It is a union of the conscious and the powerful subconscious, and of the external world of matter to our limitless energy potentials.

Most of us have difficulty relaxing our minds and bodies at the same time, except when we are asleep. If I were to tell you, "Stop all your thoughts and mental activity," you would probably tell me you couldn't. Few of us ever experience the total absence of conscious thought during periods of waking consciousness. Contrary to what you might imagine, suspension of conscious thought while you are awake is actually your entry to a purer, heightened state of consciousness. The closest most of us come to this high state of mental clarity is just before we drift into sleep. What does that tell you? That all the time we spend at our jobs or conducting our daily affairs as "alert, thinking, responsible human beings" is actually managed by a very mediocre state of our brain! The best stuff we have to work with remains unused and unknown.

Remember how the Rio Agua Clara natives sat in front of their fire and waterfall to "See the unseen and hear the unheard?" They were simply tapping into that part of brain and mind that they knew they could elicit *perfect love* energy, which can be lost in the tedium of daily existence. You and I are wise to follow their example.

Passive Awareness

This state of mind that the natives tapped, and we in our world usually ignore, is a bountiful reservoir for self-empowerment. Of the four different levels of brain wave activity we move in and out of each day, the state of Alpha is the only one in which we are passively aware. It is the only state of consciousness that allows

"Be still and know that 'I AM' GOD."

42

us to register both external and internal stimuli, thus facilitating the critical connection between self and environment that is the key to behavior transformation and motivation. The diagram below shows the four brain wave states. (Diagram, "Brain waves," derived from *Alphagenics*, p. 5.)

The path to Alpha is always achieved voluntarily.

Figure 1 - Four Brain Wave States

BRAIN WAVES	EXPERIENCES Physical & Emotional	GRAPH OF BRAIN WAVES
BETA: ——— 14 to 30 cycles per second	**AWAKE STATE**: fully alert physically active excitement fear tension anxiety	
ALPHA: ——— 8 to 13 cycles per second	**PRE-DROWSINESS**: passive awareness composure pleasant mood deep relaxation of mind and body numbness of body	
THETA: ——— 4 to 7 cycles per second	**DROWSINESS**: deep tranquility euphoric mood very deep relaxation often unconscious	
DELTA: ——— .05 to 3.5 cycles per second	**DEEP SLEEP STATE**: total unawareness unconsciousness sleep	

As you will notice from the descriptions in the second column of the diagram, Alpha is the only state in which our conscious and subconscious minds are both in play. *In each of the other states, we are unable to integrate our mind in this way.* Research has shown that while in Alpha, we are capable of accelerated learning, increased creativity, memory improvement, healing psychosomatic illness, and even extrasensory perception (ESP). Learning how to enter Alpha on your own and making time for it every day may well give you the self-improvement you are seeking!

What exactly is passive awareness? It is a state in which our thoughts are inactive — we are unaffected by sensory experiences or environmental stimulation. However, *we continue to think,* holding a single focus with a different kind of clarity than that which we are used to in our Beta mind state. For example, if you were in Alpha and passively aware, and someone came along and pinched your arm, you would feel the pinch but not try to analyze how or why it had occurred. In Beta, a fully active and aware state, you would sit up and analyze who came to pinch you and why. We avoid analysis in Alpha. If you were to listen to a symphony, you would take in the harmonious effect of the music rather than train your attention from the horn section to the string section or try to rearrange your cupboards while the music played in your living room.

At first, moving into Alpha and becoming passively aware takes some effort. You will be deliberately "blocking" sounds, distractions, and various flittings of your mind. But with practice the process becomes more and more natural. Like Ag'nike and her natives were able to do within minutes of sitting in front of the waterfall, you, too, will learn to relax quickly and completely, and then to concentrate on a single idea.

Your Senses

Biofeedback has shown that our *responses* to stimuli will block our path to Alpha much more rapidly than the stimuli themselves. Normally, the sound of heavy traffic outside would be more distracting than the low hum of the refrigerator in your kitchen, but if you choose to focus your concentration on the refrigerator while blocking out the traffic, the refrigerator will be the dominant sound you hear.

While in Alpha, because we are able to maintain single-minded concentration, distractions that occur around us become meaningless and unimportant. Therefore, it is our own interrupted concentration more than the distraction itself that moves us in and out of Alpha. The Rio Agua Clara natives could tune out the sounds of their children playing. I was able to block even distracting natural sounds of the environment after three sessions at the waterfall with the guidance of Ag'nike. So, as you practice the Alpha rituals in this book, don't expect to eliminate sensory stimuli around you. Instead, *withdraw* from all your senses: Allow these distractions to recede and become temporarily unimportant, and enjoy your heightened mind state.

There are often times when "single-minded" is necessary.

Being "Open"

Once you are able to achieve a state of Alpha, your openness to suggestion will influence the rate at which you make progress with the self-transformation rituals offered in this book. Everyone is "open" to a certain degree — some more than others. The advertising industry continually plays on the public's susceptibility to its gimmicks — package design, slogans, jingles and the models and celebrities featured in their advertising. In all aspects of our lives (not only as shoppers),

Paradise is where you learn to trust yourself first. Then you can trust others.

we make decisions based on all kinds of criteria. Some of us rely more on emotional responses; others give each issue careful thought. Those of us who are "thinkers" tend to be more resistant to suggestion and less "open"; those of us who make choices impulsively are generally less resistant and more "open."

Living with the Rio Agua Clara natives taught me much about openness. Most of these people were highly suggestible. They had no real reason not to be. Imagine their community of trust and love — no pressure from greedy marketers, no blaring television commercials, no billboards, and no need ever to lock a door! In our society we are always on our guard. We train ourselves to stay in Beta, where we can remain alert to protect ourselves from a constant barrage of intrusive and pressuring stimuli. If the natives' life sounds like paradise — it is. We may not be able to bask in the level of trust that they enjoy, but we can still learn to be open and suggestible to those influences that make us strong. The following questionnaire (facing page) will help you gauge your own level of suggestibility.

Being "open" is your confidence and freedom from all fear.

Add up the numbers you circled. The total is your suggestibility score. Refer to the Suggestibility Scale below to determine your level of suggestibility. For example, if you scored 75, your suggestibility level is medium to high. If you scored 38, your suggestibility level is low to medium. The scale will also give you an idea of how open or resistant you are likely to be to the Alpha ritual self-transformation programming.

Very Low Suggestibility

If you have scored 18 or less, you are resistant to opening up and will require to follow the suggestions in the "Low Suggestibility" section.

Figure 2 - Suggestibility Assertion List

Select the following assertions honestly. Circle the number that fits you best, and reflects what you think of yourself — NOT what other people think of you. The numbers after the assertions represent the level of your assertion.

4 — Yes, always, almost always
3 — Sometimes
0 — No, never, almost never

The question is "What do I really think about myself?"

1.	I am a sensitive woman.	0	3	4
2.	I enjoy reading novels.	0	3	4
3.	I believe in faith healing.	0	3	4
4.	I am easily influenced by others.	0	3	4
5.	I have a good imagination.	0	3	4
6.	I am emotionally moved by movies.	0	3	4
7.	I think I am self-conscious.	0	3	4
8.	I crave attention from others.	0	3	4
9.	I question myself.	0	3	4
10.	I worry too much.	0	3	4
11.	I have some fears.	0	3	4
12.	I usually give in to arguments.	0	3	4
13.	I enjoy works of art.	0	3	4
14.	I believe I am creative.	0	3	4
15.	I make decisions impulsively.	0	3	4
16.	I like bright colors.	0	3	4
17.	I lose my temper easily.	0	3	4
18.	I become very jealous at times.	0	3	4
19.	I am easily excited.	0	3	4
20.	I experience depression.	0	3	4
21.	I accept ideas too quickly.	0	3	4
22.	My feelings are easily hurt.	0	3	4
23.	I have some phobias.	0	3	4
24.	I feel afraid in the dark.	0	3	4
25.	I have difficulty making decisions.	0	3	4

TOTAL SCORE:

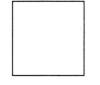

47

Figure 3 - Suggestibility Scale

0 to 18 Very Low	19 to 50 Low to Medium	51 to 80 Medium to High	81 to 100 Very High

Low to Medium Suggestibility

If your score of the Suggestibility Scale is low to medium (19 to 50), you are probably an analytical woman who exercises caution, and is to some degree emotionally cool or reserved in her behavior toward others. You may be a perfectionist who is extremely competent at whatever task you undertake. These are all positive attributes, but as far as your self-empowerment rituals are concerned, you may have some difficulty entering into a state of Alpha and sustaining passive awareness comfortably. Your natural resistance is a defense mechanism or character trait you have developed which will probably hinder your ability to "store" your self-empowerment affirmations in your memory for later use. All this means is that you may need to spend extra time with your Alpha rituals. Take special notice of the assertions for which you circled number "4." A little less rigidity in these areas will go a long way toward loosening you up! The more open and "loose" you become with yourself and the world around you, the better results your self-empowerment program will have. Self-empowerment Alpha rituals are all about opening up — becoming more trusting and positive so as to access the enormous reservoir of *perfect love* energy all around us that can, if we draw from it, truly transform the quality of our lives.

Trust yourself. God's spirit is always in you.

48

Medium to High Suggestibility

If you scored between 51 and 80 on the Suggestibility Scale, you will probably find it easy to put Alpha self-empowerment to use. You may be imaginative, gregarious, opinionated and motivated, but you may also be a little controlling, coming across "too strong" for the likes of those who don't know you. Fear not — you will easily learn to re-program your body and mind to work on those issues you want to change and to bring about the self-improvement you desire.

Very High Suggestibility

If your score is over 80, you are highly sensitive and will have no trouble at all entering Alpha and taking advantage of all it has to offer you. High sensitivity, however, may work to your detriment as it makes us vulnerable to illness, anxiety, depression and mood swings. As a woman of high sensitivity, you may have psychic awareness that you do or don't yet know about, and you may also be extremely creative, artistic, warm and extroverted.

If you find the loose character descriptions above do not fit you at all, don't worry. The point of the Suggestibility Scale is to gauge how you may respond to self-empowerment Alpha exercises, and whether or not you will need extra time with your rituals to notice results.

Your trusting soul will open powerful psychic universal energies.

"I AM"

LOVE

My *Perfect Love* Energy
is the
Vibration Energy
that brings
Harmony and Balance
to My
Spirit, Mind and Body

CHAPTER

The Path of the Alpha Ritual

Self-empowerment is the result of mastery over spirit, mind and body. Mastery of these three elements may sound as unattainable to you as the idea of becoming a millionaire, but you will be surprised that if you begin with your body and learn to tune into and regulate its energies, you will find yourself becoming more in touch with your spirit and mind.

The path to Alpha is a trip where you leave everything behind. You take nothing, not even your ego.

One of our greatest physical handicaps is our inability to relax. By "relaxation," I do not mean watching TV, visiting friends or riding the exercise bike at the gym. These are forms of recreation which serve to distract us mentally for short periods of time. They can temporarily alleviate stress, but they do little to create lasting serenity.

True relaxation is total rest for both mind and body. Total relaxation does not mean being asleep—you are awake and relaxed at the same time, aligning the energies of the body with the energies of the mind. *Symmetrical relaxation* (keeping your spine erect but not rigid) allows you to align your energies and stave off the drowsiness that will put you to sleep. Experiment with your ability to relax in the various positions and choose the one that works best for you. If sitting in a chair or on the floor doesn't work at first, begin by lying on your back with your arms at your sides. As you grow more used to symmetrical relaxation, you will be able to achieve it sitting up.

Essential to your self-empowerment Alpha rituals are: 1) a quiet setting, and 2) making time for a 20- to 30-minute session every morning and evening. Try not to force relaxation or analyze your progress. Remember that your rituals are not about conscious effort or keeping your mind in its Beta state. You are trying to release mind and body to achieve passive awareness in Alpha.

I cannot emphasize enough that if you worry about your success, attempt to evaluate your progress, or try to force yourself into Alpha, you will be working against your goal. Keep in mind that Ag'nike and the other native women accepted *perfect love* in Alpha and Alpha-consciousness shifting simply by faith. They did not analyze. Unlike other areas of endeavor, practicing your rituals requires *no conscious effort*. It may seem paradoxical, but the rule of thumb for self-transformation in Alpha is *relaxation* — a complete and total release of your mind and body. I have been teaching self-empowerment rituals for many years. When I introduced the *perfect love* philosophy I had learned from the South American natives, I found my clients progressed even faster. Learning to tap your *perfect love* and put it to use for yourself while in Alpha may dramatically change your life. To begin, I suggest you carefully follow the instructions on the succeeding pages. Once you are comfortable with the Basic Relaxation

Ritual that will let you feel what the state of Alpha is like, you can modify it to suit your own spirit, mind and body self-improvement themes.

This chapter will take you through your first Basic Relaxation Ritual. You will experience the Alpha mental state — not necessarily for the first time, but with the knowledge that you are actually doing so. Once you can comfortably enter Alpha, you can apply the "I AM" affirmations in Part Three of this book to specific issues in your life. For instance, if you are chronically depressed, are fighting overweight, or have a problem with self-confidence, I have created specific self-empowerment programs to help you. You will also learn how to create and use your own personal "I AM" affirmations for any other issues you may want to overcome. *Perfect love* applications are universal once you can enter and sustain your Alpha state with ease.

Change your thoughts and you change how you feel. Go ahead, try it now!

It is important to realize that the ritual exercise into a state of Alpha is not a form of self-hypnosis. Hypnosis is a state of *somnambulism* — the body being active while the mind is in theta. In traditional hypnosis, you give your power away to someone else who is able to tell you what to think and do. While it is said that one never does under hypnosis what one wouldn't do while conscious, if enough misinformation is given to a hypnotic subject, she will do just about anything — in the belief that what she is doing is right. My own personal and professional belief is that achieving self-transformation through Alpha is far preferable to doing so through hypnosis (Theta), because *you and only you are in control of yourself.* In Alpha you remain aware, not asleep, and are the master of your own program and progress.

Please don't be fooled into believing that you are powerless or others have more power than you do. Self-empowerment is yours for the asking.

To reach a state of Alpha, your brain waves must slow down to approximately 13-8 cycles per second. If

Figure 4 - Alpha Path Chart

Meter Level	Brain Waves	Your Mental & Physical Consciousness State
100	Beta (30-14 cycles per second)	Extreme awareness, conscious of all surroundings, rapid thought.
90	Beta	Aware of self, exercising opinions and judgment.
80	Beta	Mind wandering while thinking.
70	Beta	Beginning to let go, feeling more relaxed.
60	Beta	Becoming passively focused, less aware of surroundings.
55	Beta	Last stage of active consciousness, passive awareness taking hold.
50	Alpha (13-8 cycles per second)	Releasing body feelings, sensory withdrawal.
40	Alpha	Entering your "higher" consciousness (inaccessible in Beta).
30	Alpha	Full passive awareness, very relaxed and calm.
25	Alpha (8 cycles per second)	Complete peacefulness, very secure and centered, higher consciousness, open to programming.
20	Theta (7-4 cycles per second)	Drowsiness.
15	Delta (3.5-.5 cycles per second)	First sleep stage (unawake).
10	Delta	Middle sleep stage.
0	Delta (0.5 cycles per second)	Deep sleep stage, you are not conscious.

on a scale of 0 to 100 we put optimal Beta alertness at 100 (30-14 cycles), the level you want to reach for passive aware Alpha relaxation would be 25. The question is, how does one get there? Figure 4 (page 54), shows levels of mental and physical alertness and their corresponding positions on a 0 to 100 scale.

Avoid concern. The way of the path is easily followed.

As you go through your Basic Relaxation Ritual, you will descend through levels of consciousness toward "*Alpha level 25.*" You and your mind will govern your descent. The visualizations you can experiment with are discussed below. You will most likely begin from a fully alert Beta level of 90 to 100 as you settle down in your quiet corner for your first Basic Relaxation Ritual. Perhaps the thought of your session alone will put you at a semi-relaxed Beta level 75. As you shift down from your Beta alertness and continue on the consciousness path to Alpha, you will feel increasing composure, tranquility and relaxation. The more you relax, the less actively aware you will be of your body feelings and your senses. Single thoughts will take on greater significance, unimpeded by extraneous information. You are entering your "higher" consciousness. You will begin to feel a heightened sense of clarity and well-being. This is passive awareness in its full glory — a state in which you are open, receptive, loving and secure. Beyond a shadow of any doubt, it is the best state in which to work on yourself.

"Alpha 25" is a state where you easily absorb *perfect love* energy.

Your First Self-Empowerment Alpha Path Exercise

Let's begin. Make yourself comfortable in the place and time you have chosen for your Alpha rituals.

1. Close your eyes and imagine that you are in a grassy meadow beside a pretty, running stream. See

your reflection in the clean, crystal water of the stream. Lean over your reflection. Say to it, *"I love you." Think to yourself, "I am loving myself perfectly."* Ag'nike and the natives at the waterfall first and foremost confirmed their love for themselves before they began their meditation ritual. Say to yourself, *"Any good change that will come will come from the essence of my perfect love* energy." Breathe deeply and feel the truth and conviction of that statement.

Loving yourself is loving God and others. This will open your spiritual eyelids so that you may see the unseen on the path to Alpha.

2. Keep your eyes closed. Now imagine looking up into the sky at soft, white clouds. You see yourself in the clouds, floating on a bed of soft feathers. You are at consciousness level 100. Lie back on the featherbed and let out your breath. Relax your body into the softness of the down. The featherbed begins to descend, cradling you solidly and comfortably. You don't have to do a thing. You are perfectly safe and relaxed. Take a deep breath and let it out very slowly.

3. Allow your body to relax. There are many celestial levels below you, all marked with numbered clouds. The numbers decrease by increments of "5." As you release tension from your body and you become more relaxed, you begin to feel your gradual, comfortable descent on the featherbed through space. You are passing consciousness level 90. Hold your breath and count to 5. As you do so, tell yourself your arms and legs are becoming heavy with relaxation. Pause for a moment and feel your body. It is becoming limp and heavy all over. You continue to descend. (If you have difficulty visualizing space and clouds, imagine the levels dropping on the path of consciousness chart as you come down. A marker on the chart passes 90, going steadily downward.) Take another deep breath and hold it to the count of 5. Exhale slowly. Allow the air to completely leave your body. The level continues to

Visualize the "Alpha Path Chart" on page 48. Allow the numbers to drop as you become more and more relaxed.

drop down to 85 ...... and then down to 80. Say to yourself, "My body is becoming heavy and limp and relaxed." Concentrate on relaxation. The level drops down to 75 ...... then 70 ...... down, down, down ...... to 65.

You relax more and more with each moment. Take a deep breath and hold it to the count of 5. Exhale very slowly. Your body is settling down more and more. As you settle down, you continue to relax. The more you relax, the more comfortable you feel. Everything is very pleasant and safe as you drift down into deeper relaxation and closer to Alpha. You feel wonderful all over.

You are relaxing all your muscles, all your nerves and cells. You are entering level 60 ...... then 55. Tell yourself, "I am relaxing more and more and more." Your consciousness level drops lower and lower ...... to 50 ...... 45 ...... 40.

From the tips of your toes to the top of your head you feel very relaxed. Every part of your body is relaxing and feeling comfortable and wonderful. As you relax deeply, you avoid analyzing your feelings. You do not think about anything. You remain focused on letting go and relaxing as you descend to level 35. Soon you will become totally unaware of your environment.

Continue to tell yourself you are relaxing more and more deeply. The only thought you have is that you feel completely confident and secure. You are in a very deep state of relaxation. You are breathing rhythmically. Think to yourself, "My breathing is slower and slower." Focus on your breathing. With each breath in and each breath out, you relax more and more deeply. As you do this, you become less aware of your surroundings and how your body feels.

4. Now vividly imagine yourself, while a large autumn leaf breaks free of its branch and is gently float-

ing down. Like the leaf, you too are loose and free from all active thinking. Focus on the image of the leaf floating down ...... down ...... down. You are at *"Alpha level 30"* ...... a beautiful, deep, relaxed state. You begin to feel the peacefulness of *perfect love* energy. Your mind and body are becoming so very relaxed ...... you are at *"Alpha level 28"* ...... floating down ...... down ...... feeling relaxed and peaceful ...... to level 27 ...... 26 ...... loose and relaxed, ... now you are at *"Alpha level 25."* This is where you want to be — a deep and perfect state of passive awareness of *"Alpha 25."* Say to yourself the following suggestions, "Each time I begin my Alpha ritual path exercise, I will relax quickly and deeply. With each session I will relax more quickly than the time before. I enjoy my Self-Empowerment Ritual. They are pleasant and very satisfying. It is good to take the time every day to relax and unveil my *perfect love* energy. While in Alpha, I allow my mind to receive my "I AM" self-empowerment affirmations. I become balanced in my spirit, my mind and my body."

5. You may now continue with your self-styled Alpha programming, which I explain in Chapters 5 through 10. Insert your personal affirmations here:

You become this beautiful autumn leaf, gently floating down the Alpha path.

Your "I AM" affirmations are the most powerful. They come from within your spirit.

_____

_____

_____

_____

_____

and include the following: "My self-empowerment affirmations are to help me become better and better every day. I listen to them and take them into my mind, my body. They become what I AM. They manifest my *perfect love* energy, which heals my life as I live each day. I recognize and use my *perfect love* energy to feel better and better every day."

"While in Alpha, I will allow my mind to become susceptible to instructions which I will be giving myself. I always begin by embracing love for myself. I also associate my body and mind states to the Alpha level number 25. By simply thinking, *"Alpha level 25,"* my mind and body will respond and I will quickly enter into *"Alpha level 25."*

"Each time I begin my Alpha ritual exercise, I relax quickly and deeply and reach *'Alpha level 25.'* With each session, I relax and reach Alpha more quickly than the time before. I enjoy my self-empowerment Alpha exercise.

6. To leave your state of Alpha and return to full alertness in Beta, you begin to count slowly — by increments of "10" — from level 25 to level 95. As you say the number "35," you begin to feel more aware. Say to yourself, "I continue to manifest my *perfect love* energy as I become aware of my surroundings. As I move higher — through awareness, I feel self-confident and comfortable all over. When I have reached level 100, I will feel totally alert and actively aware of my surroundings. I am pleased with myself and enthusiastic about my life and my goals."

Count up to 45 ...... 55 ...... 65. Say to yourself, "I am becoming more aware of my environment and my body." Moving up to 75 ...... "As I become more aware, I remain comfortably relaxed and composed. I am alert and peaceful." Going up to 85 ...... 95 ...... "As I open my eyes, I become fully aware. I feel wonderful and comfortable all over." You have reached the end of your self-empowerment Alpha exercise.

Trust in God's understanding, the way of the Alpha path will be made clear and easy to follow.

Read through the Alpha Path Exercise several times so you understand its stages and the different levels of consciousness through which you will travel. Imagine yourself descending and relaxing into Alpha. Does the language in this book feel right to you? If not, change it. Make it fit who you are. If memorizing or becoming familiar enough with the whole process seems too daunting a task at first, make a tape recording of your own voice counting you down through the consciousness Alpha path levels. Add your individual affirmations, as well. Count yourself back up to Beta on the tape. You can also have a friend guide you through the ritual as she reads to you the instructions from this book.

Advanced Alpha Method

You will find that you will not need your tape or a friend after only a few practice sessions. The wonderful thing about experiencing Alpha is that it soon becomes second nature to us. Reaching *"Alpha 25"* is easier each time. After a short while, you may not even need the countdown process at all: Focus on the thought of *"Alpha level 25,"* and you will drop downward through the mind states on your own, feeling the free, floating mental and physical effects of deep Alpha in a matter of a few moments.

The principle and reason by which you can achieve rapid descent into Alpha is the same principle that worked for Ag'nike and the natives. Staring at the waterfall or into the flames of the fire, the natives were associating the vision of the water and flames with a state of total passive awareness. They could enter Alpha within three minutes. You will be able to learn this quick induction just as easily. All it takes is practice — letting the mind connect a cue (which can be an image or the words *"Alpha 25"*) with a response. Psychologists call this "behavioral conditioning." Eventually, by simply thinking of the cue *"Alpha level 25"* and visualizing the leaf floating gently through the air, your body will automatically begin to put itself into the state you have come to associate with that cue.

You can easily invite the level of "Alpha 25," after you have learned the way of the path.

How do you know you are truly in Alpha? In Chapter 4 of this book, I offer specific "body-feedback tests" you can use for confirmation. Once you are in Alpha, however, you will experience the following:

- A state of higher consciousness.
- A passive-aware detachment from your surroundings.
- *"Perfect love* energy" as a completely natural feeling or thought.
- A oneness with your higher power or God.
- The strength of "I AM."
- The empowerment to create what is good for you and the universe.
- *Perfect love* for yourself.

All of the above should feel natural and comfortable. Acknowledgment of these principles and thoughts is the doorway to self-transformation.

"I AM"

At This Very Moment
Empowered to
Make
the Perfect Decision

CHAPTER

Successful Alpha Feedback (Self-Regulation Exercises)

When you are able to practice Self-Empowerment Alpha Rituals successfully, you will probably be curious to know whether you are actually achieving the Alpha state. I designed a method I call Successful Alpha Feedback (self-regulation exercises) which I use with all my clients to help them become more confident with use the of Self-Empowerment Alpha Rituals. The self-regulation exercises gives you several Successful Alpha Feedback examples to improve your success with your perfect love rituals. The Successful Alpha Feedback self-regulation method is a natural way for you to review how well you are progressing. Everyone wants to know how well they are doing and since I can't be with you in person, the following examples will help you to appreciate the empowerment you have to influence changes in your own body.

Daily claiming your self-empowerment will increase your self-confidence and self-esteem.

When you are in "Alpha level 25" state, you experience an energy shift of your conscious state. You have already read in the preceding chapters, that while in Alpha, you are capable of mind and body control. You can measure your success to influence your body functions by some of the feedback results you obtain while practicing your self-empowerment Alpha rituals. When you are successful with any one of the Alpha Feedback self-regulation exercises, you may assume that you are successfully experiencing the *"Alpha level 25."*

Remember, your success comes from your *perfect love* energy.

Remember, your ultimate objective is successfully achieving the *"Alpha level 25,"* and acknowledging your self-empowerment. Your focus should not be merely on your ability to succeed with *"Alpha level 25."* That is only one step along the pathway to reaching a self empowerment of your spirit, mind and body. Avoid concern about your progress. Remember that you are successful because of your quiet passive awareness and your effortless attitude. You cannot force progress in the Self-Empowerment Alpha Rituals.

There are six Alpha self-regulation exercises which you may use in order to appraise your progress in achieving self-empowerment of your mind and body. The six self-regulation exercises are self-empowerment of regulating your:

- 1 Pulse Rate
- 2 Respiration
- 3 Glands
- 4 Muscles
- 5 Temperature
- 6 Emotions

You may have better results with some self-regulation exercises than with others. Avoid emphasizing the results of any particular exercise. Often very successful women have poor results with one or two of the exercises.

These example self-regulation exercises are merely guides to aid you in your evaluation of your Self-Empowerment Alpha Ritual state. Take your time as you begin each exercise. Be certain that you have carefully followed the Self-Empowerment Alpha Ritual path and that you are in *"Alpha level 25."* Avoid worry or concern of any kind. Be mindful that the *"Alpha level 25"* is an effortless state of consciousness. It is important for you to understand that the mind in Alpha will not harm you. Should you have any reservations, discuss your Self-Empowerment Alpha Ritual program with your physician before you begin. You should be free from concern about the Self-Empowerment Alpha Ritual sessions. The only way to practice the Self-Empowerment Alpha Ritual is with *confidence in the program, perfect love, faith in yourself and high belief in your success.*

Self-Regulation Exercise 1: Pulse Rate

In this first self-regulation exercise you demonstrate your ability to regulate your pulse rate by lowering it. Before you begin the Self-Empowerment Alpha Ritual session, take a reading of your pulse and record it. Using the advance Self-Empowerment Alpha Ritual session on page 60, enter into what you feel to be *"Alpha level 25."* When you have reached this level, you will be able to achieve physical influence.

You are empowered to influence your blood system. Trust your positive thoughts.

Begin concentrating on your circulatory system. Think of the blood as it flows through your veins. Feel your circulation throughout your entire body. Pay attention to controlling the rate of your circulation. As you feel completely relaxed, think about slowing down your circulation a little bit. Concentrate on controlling your heart beat very slightly. Thing about decreasing the activity of your entire body's functions. Feel your body resting completely. Focus on the thought of your pulse rate slowing down.

Once you feel you have sufficiently slowed down your circulatory system and lowered your pulse rate, tell yourself that when you complete your ritual session, you will have a slower pulse rate. Then begin to bring yourself back up to Beta (the active aware state) as you have learned in the advance Self-Empowerment Alpha Ritual session page 60, If you have entered a good state of *"Alpha level 25,"* you should have significantly lowered your pulse rate. You measure this change by again taking your pulse and comparing the new pulse rate with the rate you recorded before you began the ritual . This self-regulation exercise may also be reversed, — meaning you can also increase the rate of your pulse.

Self-Regulation Exercise 2: Respiration

You are the master of your spirit, mind and body. You will relax and breathe easily.

In the self-regulation exercise you show how well you can influence your breathing by lowering it. Before beginning your Self-Empowerment Alpha Ritual session, take a measurement of your respiration; count the number of times you inhale and exhale within one minute and record it. Using the advance Self-Empowerment Alpha Ritual session on page 60, enter into what you feel to be *"Alpha level 25."* Begin to concentrate on your breathing. Think of slowing down your breathing. Feel your lungs relaxing and letting go. Think about this relaxation. Gradually slow down the number of breaths you inhale and exhale. This will happen naturally because as you allow your body to rest completely, you require less oxygen and therefore your breathing rate will lower.

While you relax at *"Alpha level 25,"* you are empowered to regulate your respiration. Tell yourself that your breathing will remain slower for a brief time after you complete your Self-Empowerment Alpha Ritual session. Slowly begin to bring yourself back up to an awake Beta state as you have learned in the advance Self-Empowerment Alpha Ritual exercise. If you have successfully entered *"Alpha level 25,"* you should have lowered your respiration. As you did before the ritual session, once again count the number of times you inhale and exhale during one minute and compare this reading with the first figure.

Self-Regulation Exercise 3: Glands

A third area of your body behavior you can regulate is a glandular response to a stimuli. The gland self-regulation exercise is called the "Lemon Test Exercise." It is a useful experience for influencing the salivary gland. Using the advance Self-Empowerment Alpha Ritual session on page 60, enter into what you feel to be *"Alpha level 25."* Begin vividly to imagine yourself in the kitchen of your home. Notice the colors of the room. See the location of the cupboards, the furniture and any other objects of interest in the room. Notice every detail, even notice the clothing you are wearing. Make this scene as vivid as possible in your imagination.

Now! Imagine where you are standing in a kitchen. From where you stand you can look at the refrigerator. Look at it carefully. Walk over to it and open the door, noticing the hardness of the door handle. Make this a vivid imaginary experience. As you open the refrigerator door, feel the cool air coming from the

You are empowered to control your glands, and claim perfect health.

refrigerator. Reach into the refrigerator and pick out a lemon. The lemon is cold and moist in your hand. Close the refrigerator door and walk over to the counter.

Take a knife in your hand and feel the hardness of the handle. Holding the lemon in one hand and the knife in the other, cut the lemon in half. Notice the beads of lemon juice on the blade of the knife. Put the knife down on the counter and pick up half of the lemon. Bite into it. Feel the experience of actually biting into the lemon and tasting it. Notice the taste. Notice the reaction. Slowly bring yourself back up to an active aware Beta state as you have learned in the advance Self-Empowerment Alpha Ritual exercise. After returning to the Beta state, answer two questions, "Did you salivate?" and "Did you taste the lemon?" Nearly everyone who follows the Lemon Exercise will salivate and most people will actually experience the taste of the lemon. If you salivated, it is an indication that you have influenced your salivary gland. You now realize that you can control this gland and if you have learned to control one gland, eventually you can learn control of the other glands in your body. This potential for self regulation may be extended to your entire body.

Self-Regulation Exercise 4: Muscles

To succeed, you must be single-minded, with one thought, "my arm is light and floating."

With the fourth self-regulation exercise you demonstrate how effectively you can influence the muscles in a particular part of your body. This test involves arm levitation. Using the advance Self-Empowerment Alpha Ritual session on page 60, enter into *"Alpha level 25."*

Begin to concentrate on one of your arms. Vividly imagine that this arm is very light, it is so light that you begin to feel it floating up. Concentrate on this single idea of your arm feeling very light and floating. Vividly picture your arm floating; feel it floating. Tell yourself that your arm is so light it is floating up. Repeat to yourself several times, "My arm is light and floating." Think of your arm floating without any active effort on your part. Remaining in a completely passive aware state, you allow your arm to float. Do not resist the sensation, but permit your arm to rise up and float. Your single thought is that you are allowing your arm to float. Slowly return to the active aware Beta state. If you have entered a low Alpha state your arm will lift up and float while feeling very light. You have influenced your autonomic behavior. You have controlled your muscles and nerves in your arm in order to have your arm float up.

In practicing arm levitation you must concentrate on the arm floating for at least ten minutes after you have reached *"Alpha level 25."* Do not become discouraged if you do not achieve arm levitation immediately. Practice the exercise several times. Eventually your arm will levitate easily. As with all self-empowerment Alpha exercise, it is important that you not try to force your body. Agree in your mind to allow your arm to passively levitate. If you continue to have difficulty with this arm levitation exercise, incorporate the following vivid imaginary experience in your initiation. When you begin to imagine your arm floating, vividly picture a string tied around your wrist. Several balloons are attached to this string. Vividly see the balloons and picture their colors. See the balloons lifting up your arm as they rise and float. Feel the string pulling around your wrist. Actually feel your arm floating upwards with the balloons. Take your time, relax and be patient with this exercise and you will achieve arm levitation. After you complete your Self-Empowerment Alpha Ritual session, slowly begin to bring yourself back up to active aware Beta state.

Self-Regulation Exercise 5: Temperature

You are the master of your body temperature. You can feel warm or cool at will.

The fifth self-regulation exercise helps you demonstrate your ability to influence your body temperature. Following the advance Self-Empowerment Alpha Ritual, enter into *"Alpha level 25."* Place your hand over your abdomen. Concentrate on feeling warmth on your abdomen under your hand. Think to yourself that your abdomen is beginning to feel warm. Feel the warmth. Say to yourself, "My abdomen is becoming warm." Repeat this phrase several times as you continue to relax. Think about and notice the warmth for several minutes. The only thought you entertain is of the warm feeling which is spreading in your abdomen. Slowly bring yourself back up to the active aware Beta state as you have learned in the Self-Empowerment Alpha Ritual session on page 59-60.

In practicing this exercise, most people will experience a warm pleasurable feeling in the abdomen region. Often a woman will feel this warmth move throughout her body. This is perfectly normal and means you have very good control. If you are having difficulty managing your body temperature, add the following vivid imaginary experience during your exercise. Vividly imagine placing a heating pad on your abdomen. You have turned the temperature control up and you begin to feel the warmth of the pad. It is greater than your present body temperature. Picture the control and imagine turning the temperature even higher. You may also picture a hot water bottle and think of its warmth and weight against your abdomen. Or if you choose, imagine the sun's warmth against your body, as if you were lying on the beach. This will also help you increase your body temperature. Any one of these vivid imaginary experiences is helpful in regulating body temperature. Remember that once you reach *"Alpha level 25,"* you must concentrate for several minutes in order to experience the increased feeling of warmth.

Temperature management of your body may be demonstrated in another way. You can lower temperature in one area and increase temperature in another area. After entering *"Alpha level 25,"* think about your hands. Do not have them touching. Concentrate on one of your hands becoming warmer and the other hand feeling cooler. Imagine the hand which is warming up to be under a warm water faucet. Feel the warm water running over that hand. In the same way, picture your other hand under a cold water faucet and feel the stream of cold water running over that hand. Vividly imagine these two experiences as one hand becomes hot and the other cold. While concentrating, alternate from one hand to the other; think of one hand becoming hot for 30 seconds and then change to the other hand and think of it becoming cool for 30 seconds. Alternate in this manner several times. Practice this for five to ten minutes while you relax deeply at *"Alpha level 25."* Slowly bring yourself back up to the active aware Beta state as you have learned in the advance Self-Empowerment Alpha Ritual session. Just as soon as you become fully alert, touch your hands together. If you have been successful with temperature control, you will feel a distinct difference in the temperature of your hands.

Self-Regulation Exercise 6: Emotions

The self-regulation exercise will help you enhance your ability to be in control of your emotions. The previous exercises have involved empowerment of body functions. This exercise demonstrates your ability to be empowered of your mind/body behavior. Using the advance Self-Empowerment Alpha Ritual exercise, enter into *"Alpha level 25."* Concentrate on a feeling of sadness. Think of feeling unhappy. Remind yourself of a past sad situation. Vividly remember your emotional response when you felt this unhappiness. Actually experience the emotional feeling of sadness.

Next, concentrate on a feeling of happiness. Focus on feeling joyful. Repeat to yourself that you are very happy. As before, you increase this emotion by thinking of a time when you have felt happy. Recall something which pleases you and feel the emotional response of joy. Be sure you complete your exercise with this happy experience. Return slowly to the active aware Beta state. After this exercise, you will be able to clearly recall the alternate sensations of sadness and joy. In the same way you achieved emotional regulation with this exercise, you can also be empowered by your entire psychological behavior.

A Reminder

Self-Regulation Exercises are only one method of evaluating your self empowerment of all functions — mind and body. With the tools of the Self-Regulation Exercise, you can learn to measure and evaluate your self empowerment experiences of both your mind and your body.

"I AM"

LOVE

At This Very Moment
I Am in God's
Perfect Will

CHAPTER 5

Rehearsing Your Self-Empowerment in the Mental Theater

Emile Coué, a French healer who used auto-suggestion on his subjects in the early 1900s, said, "Our actions spring not from our will of the conscious, but from our subconscious imagination." In terms of consciousness, if imagination is the higher form, then will is the lower form. Coué went on to say, *"When the conscious will is in conflict with the subconscious imagination, the subconscious imagination always wins."*

When your "will" and imagination are together, you are empowered to create positive changes.

To Ag'nike and her villagers, the imagination was the creative force which could heal the sick and bring happiness to the melancholy. She called the imagination "thought pictures," and said that often our thought pictures were in conflict with our will. An example, is a person who is ill may wish or "will" to be well. However, the person's sincere efforts wanting and willing to get better doesn't seem to help. What is wrong? That person's imagination, Ag'nike explained, did not possess a healthy thought picture and was dominating over her will. "We must allow the thought picture to be harmonious with the will to take effect. The use of will does not matter. If the thought picture is of *perfect love* energy and wellness, then it will be so. Always remember, *'Any good change that will come, will come from the essence of perfect love* energy.'"

In my practice as a guide, I have found that the imagination (mental picture) can push people with severe problems into a state of mind where they can

Patty, avoiding crossing a log bridge.

finally begin to change and feel whole. I will give you an example from an experience with my former wife, Patty. One day Patty arrived by bus at the edge of the jungle in Colombia, S. A. to visit me. We were met by three native guides who led us on a hazardous trail back to our jungle camp. Hiking through the thick jungle growth was an obstacle course, with several primitive bridges made from fallen trees with their surface flattened by the native's machetes. Patty suffered from acrophobia (fear of heights). Whenever it was necessary for us to cross the canyon rivers, Patty's phobia would prevent her from crossing the log bridge. She would beg me to take the long way around to get to the other side, causing us to fall back behind our guides. This was the only trail back to our camp site. I asked them to wait so I could help Patty overcome her anxiety. I thought immediately about Coué's and the natives' principle *"Whenever the conscious will is in conflict with the subconscious imagination, the imagination always wins."* I realized that our actions spring not from our will, but from our imagination. I knew that if we were to get back to camp before dark, it would be necessary for Patty to change her negative imagination in order to overcome her fear of heights.

The natives and I set up a 30-foot log on a level area of the river shore. The width of the log was one foot, having one side of the surface flattened with the native's machete and made safe and comfortable to walk on. I asked Patty if she would like to walk on the log with me. Patty and I practiced walking across the log a few times. She walked behind me with her eyes closed and her hands on my shoulders. She was confident and comfortable, knowing that the ground was only a short distance away. We practiced this exercise while she was vividly imagining that there was a river about 60 feet under the log, she practiced till she felt ready and completely confident. We went to one of the crossing bridges that was 30 feet above the river. I instructed Patty to close her eyes — take a couple of deep breaths, and relax her mind and body. She began walking behind me, her eyes closed and her hands on my shoulders, imagining she was still walking on the log that was placed on the ground. She felt safe and confident, and experienced this same confidence as we walked across this

Patty and Angelo
safely leaving the jungle.

log high over the river. Patty's successful crossing was possible because she was a willing and fast learner and that she allowed her imagination to create confident and safe "thought pictures" of the event.

In the beginning, when Patty questioned her capability, she would see herself falling rather than see herself walking easily across to safety. The reason Patty could finally cross the river on the narrow log was because she transformed her subconscious mind to a positive imaginary scene which canceled the old negative image. The "will" needs a symmetrical mental picture to guide it. "Without our harmonious mental pictures, the will is powerless. In our quiet moments at the waterfall, we create lifelike thought pictures to keep us in the spirit of *perfect love* energy," Ag'nike explained to me. "Nothing else matters in those moments — only our thoughts and the pictures they make in our subconscious mind. If we conceive sad thoughts often enough, we produce subconscious sad pictures and so we experience bad feelings and sadness. If we conceive thoughts of fear and doubt often enough, we produce subconscious fear pictures and from those we suffer pain and illness. Likewise, when we have recurring thoughts of love, we create subconscious pictures of giving and receiving, and there is no fear. We feel safe and are well and happy. During the time we spent at the waterfall, we learned to create real-life thought pictures. We focused our attention first on small things and then on bigger and bigger things, and soon we are able to make lifelike pictures in our minds that include all of our surroundings."

Visualization, then, is the seed that begins all that happens in our lives. *We are what we believe ourselves to be.* We have continually "seen" or imagined ourselves that way or we would not be where we are today. Changing what we are is as simple as changing the mental pictures we have of ourselves. Remember that our existing pictures have been forming over years, and chances are that years from now those pictures will have evolved beyond what they are today. But to transform these thought pictures in a short period of time is another matter. The key to making these changes happen is the mental technique that Patty practiced to get over the log, the same technique used by Ag'nike and her natives at the waterfall. I call it *vivid visualization* — creating "lifelike" images as the Rio Agua Clara villagers did while deep in meditation. For most people in the western world, visualization remains a unintentional practice. Few of us admit to doing it because most of us don't even realize that we engage in such a thing at all. We do — much of the time — but on an unconscious level.

Therefore, practicing *active or vivid* visualization feels awkward, for we are not used to this as a conscious activity. Visualization is the principal means of conscious and subconscious communication. It is a wonderful way to "problem-solve" without analysis and conscious effort. But in our society, it has to be learned. Counseling clients over the years, I have found that teaching them to visualize is easier if we work our way up the visualization "ladder" — from first, a very small scale, to a much larger, lifelike "theater." This chapter takes you through six visualization exercises so that you, too, can learn to create your vivid mental theater in which you will see yourself acting, moving, speaking — *being* as you want to be.

Exercise 1: Simple Visualization

Place a small, simple object — perhaps a pencil — in front of you (16 to 18 inches away). Sit comfortably, relax and take several slow, deep breaths while looking at the pencil. Don't strain to focus on details; simply see the pencil as a whole. Now, as you close your

You and the actress soon become one.

eyes, keep a picture of the pencil in your mind. Don't force the picture if it doesn't come naturally. Just keep practicing the exercise until you can see a clear image of the pencil when your eyes are shut. Then practice the exercise with a different object — one that is not so basic, with more details, such as a beautiful flower or a favorite picture for you to grasp and retain.

Exercise 2: Complex Visualization

You will need to be very relaxed to do this exercise. As you rest comfortably, "see" in your mind a photo of the face of someone you know very well. Now call up photos in your mind of other people who are familiar, and continue on with places, buildings and scenes that come easily to your mind. You are training your mind to function like a camera. As you go about your daily activities, make visual "photographs" of interesting sights you come across. Collect a "library" of images. Try to call up images from your library at different times — while working, doing chores and relaxing. Do the images come into mental focus easily for you?

When you are acting, it is easy to play fearful roles.

Practice will increase your ability to recall and "bring up" your mental pictures. When you find you can vividly imagine any object, person or scene with ease, you will be ready to work on your sensory awareness.

Exercise 3: Sensory Awareness

Find a comfortable place to relax. Sit comfortably. Now, recall to memory a special place. Recall everything you felt when you were in that place. If it was the mountains, remember the smell of clean air, of pine trees, or maybe the sound of a stream. If your thoughts are of the beach, hear the surf and feel the warm sand. Now turn your imagination to a more complex scene — one with several people in it — perhaps at a friend's house or in your work place. Vividly create this scene in your mind. Feel as if you are in that room with those people right now. See all the physical details — furnishings and decorations—the view from the windows. Notice all the people in the room with you, and everything about them. Hear their voices and take in their clothing. What you are doing is setting a physical "stage." Now see and hear the activity in the room. Notice the actions of each person — what personality does he or she have? "Sense" the personalities in the room; become sensitive to behavior, moods and expressions.

By noticing so many elements at once, you are practicing what I call "multiple awareness." Your degree of mind control is expanding. The purpose of this is to allow you to regulate your emotional self with programming and vivid visualization while in Alpha. Emotion pervades and governs our entire being — mental as well as physical. Thus, self-empowerment of our emotions leads to control of much of our physical and psychological life experience.

Exercise 4: Sensory Transformation

Many of us have strong, almost uncontrollable feelings of dislike or animosity. These are destructive emotions which can interfere with our living *perfect love* more than they help us. This exercise teaches us to transfer negative feelings into positive ones.

Vividly visualize a person who you have strongly disliked in the past. Remember your feelings of animosity and vividly create once again that negative mental and emotional state. Now let your mind conjure up someone for whom you care very much. Vividly picture this person and recall all the positive, good feelings you have for this person. Feel the affection as strongly as you can and hold on to those feelings. While holding on to those positive feelings, recall the picture of the person you dislike. Transfer all the positive feelings you are holding to the disliked person. Begin to feel the polarity, opposition of feelings while vividly imagining the disliked person. Practice this even if this seems difficult at first. To reconcile polarity of emotions requires considerable effort and results are well worth it. How long does it take you to pair the good feelings with the negative image? Practice—it is healthier for you to live in *perfect love* energy than to be out of it with negative feelings that produce unhappiness and illness.

You are empowered to love the unloving. There are no limits in perfect love.

Exercise 5: Non-Specific Vision

When our eyes are open, we tend to look at things and locate definite forms. Our brain, as we do this, is usually in Beta. Alpha brain waves are best sustained with our eyes closed, but people who are good at Alpha meditation can keep their eyes open. Zen meditators can emit abundant Alpha waves with their eyes wide open. The type of *attention* we are engaging in is more important than the position of our eyelids. This exercise teaches you how to maintain Alpha while your eyes are open. You may want to absorb information more effectively while reading or studying — and this is obviously only possible when your eyes are open!

Rest comfortably in a symmetrically relaxed position (your body erect but not rigid; refer to Chapter 3). Bring yourself to "*Alpha level 25.*" Open your eyes. You are passively aware. Scan your surroundings. What are the colors and shapes? Move your eyes slowly in a wide circle, starting from the left and going toward the right. Scan slowly; avoid focusing on specific details. Reduce this circle to a circle smaller within it, again going from left to right and back to the left. Reduce this circle to still a smaller one. If you keep reducing your visual circles, your eyes will come to rest straight ahead of you. Do not focus on this spot — continue to take in your entire field of vision as you did when you first began to scan. See as much as possible without looking at details or forms. You can see to the left and right without moving your eyes or head. Scan out of the corners of your eyes, without moving your eyeballs. Take in your whole environment. Your eyes are open. You are in Alpha. You can see all around you without trying. The experience should be pleasant and relaxing. You are practicing your non-specific visual ability.

You are empowered to transform from the actress—to the real you!

Exercise 6: Specific Vision

Rest in a position of symmetrical relaxation and bring yourself to *"Alpha level 25."* Open your eyes and remain passively aware. Choose a single object in front of you. Focus on it.

As you continue to relax, scan the object in a circle as you did in the last exercise. Your scanning field will be much smaller as you are focusing only on one object. Concentrate on this object. Gaze at it without focusing on details — take it all in. Do this for several minutes. Hold your general gaze without allowing your mind to wander.

It is important to note that *scanning* stimulates Alpha brain waves, but *staring* does not. If your mind wanders, your scanning will stop and you will find yourself staring fixedly at particular details instead. Continue scanning.

Visualization is a learned skill. Don't be discouraged if you feel you can't do it properly at first. Relax. Play with pictures. Daydream. "See" people and places in your mind as you drift to sleep. Let yourself grow familiar with the new "movie camera" you have put in your head. Then do the exercises and see what happens. Remember, Ag'nike and her friends daily visited the waterfall.

Mental Theater

Here you can discover ways to see the unseen and hear the unheard.

Vivid visualization on a lifelike scale — "seeing" yourself as you would if watching a movie or play — is known as *mental theater,* and is a critically important part of your self-transformation exercises and I AM affirmations. I strongly encourage you to use mental theater in *all* your self-empowerment rituals.

When you practice mental theater, your imagination creates vivid mental pictures. You can use this imaginary exercise in two ways: 1) putting yourself in the role of spectator of the mental-theater scene, known as *objective mental* theater, or 2) involving yourself as a *participant* in the mental-theater scene, known as virtual reality mental theater.

Because of the lifelike nature of the scenes you "see," when you practice mental theater, you will feel your senses and emotions responding as they do to real events. This is why I use the term "virtual reality." Your nightly dreams are another form of virtual reality, but they differ from mental theater because you are sleeping and not in control. Self-empowerment mental theater keeps you conscious, in harmony with your visualizations and thoughts, and in control.

You can choose to be a *spectator* or a *participant* in your mental-theater exercises and you can practice the exercises by *self-suggestion, suggestion by another person, or using a pre-recorded tape.*

Objective Mental Theater

To watch yourself on a make-believe "stage" may be an easier way to begin. Some women, whose real-life counterpart is unpleasant or frightening, find it difficult to conduct an imaginary exercise. Feeling anxiety in the Alpha state creates distraction and may even re-inforce your existing problem. Practice mental theater remaining as calm and relaxed as possible. Continued practice after awhile will make this easier.

The power of the mental theater has no limits.

To use objective mental theater, vividly imagine an experience taking place. Re-create an experience you have had in your own life, but one in which you are not directly involved in the situation. You are only a *spectator* of the action. Picture someone very much like you — *but not you* — on the stage of your imaginary mental theater. It will be much easier for you to observe another person — not you — in a difficult situation that causes you anxiety. Practice being the spectator until you feel comfortable.

Once you are able to be a spectator in your mental theater without feeling anxiety, you can progress to virtual-reality mental theater and become an active scene participant. The exercises in this book are intended to allow you to grow comfortable with your own process of self-transformation, so approach your issues gradually and work on them by degree. Like each droplet of Ag'nike's waterfall, we are ever-changing in small ways.

Example: You are easily intimidated by authority figures (a parent, employer, celebrity, in-law, brother or sister, relative, men, bankers, corporate heads, police, etc.) You can use objective mental theater to help you overcome this fear.

Follow the consciousness path (Basic Relaxation Ritual, Chapter 3) to *"Alpha level 25."* Now create your imaginary scene. Picture yourself entering a theater which you have been in before. You can clearly recall its details. Remember the seats, recall any decorations and think about the last time you were in that particular theater. As you look at the stage in front of you, see the curtain, which remains closed.

When you have a clear picture of the theater and you can "feel" its environment, imagine yourself sitting down. Choose a seat where you sat before. As you gaze at the stage, the curtain opens. An actress walks forward. She resembles you very closely — she could be your twin. While you know this woman is not you, you are able to identify with her because she is so much like you. You will observe all her experiences, but because you are a spectator, you will feel no anxiety or discomfort yourself.

The actress is going to put herself through an experience you have had before — a situation that made you very intimidated and uncomfortable. The stage is a cross-section of a room. It is a room in which you once had a very negative experience. But because it is not you in the room this time, you feel no anxiety.

The actress enters the room and closes the door behind her. She stands talking to another person. She is confident and sure of herself. Because she is so confident, you feel yourself identifying with her. You are observing that it is quite possible to feel sure of yourself while facing someone of authority. In your men-

It is always much easier to watch *others* play a difficult role.

86

tal-theater exercise, each time you imagine this scene, you are quicker to feel the actress's confidence as she stands in front of this authority figure. The actress is so much like you that you begin to see yourself in her place. Each time you do this exercise, it becomes easier for you to identify with her.

Soon you are able to easily see yourself in the shoes of your look-alike. You, too, are on stage, entering the room, feeling empowered and confident.

After several mental-theater exercises, the spectator role will become easy. You will have mastered the feelings of watching the experience while remaining controlled and comfortable. You will have begun to *project yourself* into the actual experience. At this point you are ready to progress to virtual-reality mental theater.

Virtual-Reality Mental Theater

This exercise works well if you can easily plunge into an imagined scene without any intimidation or discomfort. You will "see" yourself actively participating in the lifelike scene you observed in the exercise before. You will feel all the emotions as you engage in the experience since it is you up there on the stage, not an actress. Because you are directly involved in your imaginary mental theater, your programming will be extremely effective. As you keep re-enacting an experience, you can also re-program yourself with your own affirmation.

Virtual reality is very much like a real dream.

Example: You are easily intimidated in the presence of authority figures (a parent, employer, celebrity, in-law, brother or sister, relative, men, bankers, corporate heads, police, etc.) Virtual-reality mental theater helps you overcome your fear.

87

Bring yourself down the consciousness path to *"Alpha level 25."* Now create your imaginary scene. Picture yourself on the stage of the theater. You are not the audience, as you were in your objective mental theater — you are on the very same stage that you watched the actress perform who looked just like you. Take the time to clearly envision the stage around you—it is the room you are familiar with and in front of you is the authority figure.

Walk around the set. See, feel, sense and recognize every detail of the surroundings. Now turn and face the person you need to speak to who is in authority. Feel yourself empowered, confident, self-assured.

The scene is clear and vivid. You see the room's furnishings and decorations — the different colors. You smell the room around you. You are standing and talking to the person in authority. You can hear the serious, important conversation that is going on. You realize you are this person's match — you are feeling very sure of yourself. You allow the conversation to continue so that you can reinforce and enjoy the empowering experience.

You can virtually experience a menacing scene, without ever feeling the fear in you.

Begin to believe that when you are in any situation that previously intimidated you, you will feel empowered and very confident. There is nothing to fear. Your mental-theater exercise has made you clear and strong.

Repeating Your Mental-Theater Exercises

In all the following chapters, you are encouraged to use mental theater in your self-empowerment rituals. You will find that any self-improvement program works better when you combine mental theater exercise with specific affirmations. You are actually combining two stimuli — imaginary experience and affirmations — and this makes all your rituals more effective.

Patience is very important. As you have learned from Ag'nike's waterfall ritual, it takes practice to use these methods effectively. Some women must work harder at vivid visualization and mental theater techniques. Practice makes them much easier, so give yourself a few weeks to feel comfortable and connected with these methods.

Methods of Suggestion

Repeating your "I AM" affirmations in combination with positive imaginary experiences is the core of the self-empowerment program you are learning. You may use *self-suggestion* or *outside suggestion* in making your affirmations.

Self-Suggestion

Determine how long you wish to practice your Alpha exercise. Beginners should allow 30 minutes per session. When you are familiar with the ritual path, you will be able to shorten the sessions to 15 or 20 minutes. Be careful not to make your sessions too brief. Hurried sessions will only create more tension and distraction in your life, and sessions that are too long, can cause you fatigue.

Write down the affirmations you want to use. Remember to be concise and use only positive terminology. Study your affirmations and reduce them to a few key words. The more concise you are, the more easily you will recall them. You do not want to engage in active thought while you are in Alpha.

Outside Suggestion

"Outside suggestion" simply means that you use a pre-recorded tape. To compose an effective tape, use affirmations that are meaningful and personal to you. Start with the script in Chapter 3 (Basic Relaxation Ritual) that takes you down the consciousness path. Then record the specific "I AM" affirmations you have chosen for the issues you wish to tackle. If you choose to have someone else record your affirmations, it is important that she is very familiar with all the dynamics of Alpha exercises, and that you are completely comfortable with her voice and its rhythms and inflections. As with all your ritual exercises, choose a comfortable place in which to practice your programming.

In the following chapters, many I AM affirmations are supplied as a starting point for your own program affirmations. The program you create will only work if you accept and cooperate with your affirmations. Repeat the exercise continuously. Though outside suggestion makes your Alpha exercises relatively simple, still you must be patient and consistent with your program.

Your Self-Empowerment "I AM" Affirmations

The sample "I AM" affirmations in the following chapters will help you create your own effective self-empowerment programs and tape recordings. These I AM affirmations have been carefully screened and modified throughout my years of working with women on their self-empowerment. Feel free to change words or phrases to increase the meaning for you, but follow the general suggestions in creating your own Alpha script. You may choose to combine certain phrases; this is fine as long as your affirmations do not become too complicated. The use of the personal address "I AM" is exactly as it is stated, you are all that you are through your spirit that connects to the spirit of God. "I AM" is significant because there is no other than "I AM." You will learn the meaning and power of the "I AM" affirmations as they help you to become the real you — the "I AM." I cannot stress strongly enough the importance of personalized "I AM" affirmations. If you find the language of an affirmation unpleasant or unnatural, you will not respond to that affirmation. Only you are the judge of the effect an affirmation has on you. You must discover this for yourself.

In the Old Testament when God was asked His name, he said "I AM" that I AM."

Use words you find pleasant and acceptable. "I AM" affirmations should be positive. Draw on the wealth of "I AM." For example, "I AM empowered to succeed." "I AM confident in the work I do." "I AM *perfect love* energy." Be comfortable with your affirmations and make them what you want yourself to be.

Above all, always begin by accepting your *perfect love* energy and *totally love and accept yourself.* This is your launching pad for harmony and change.

Part Three

Self-Empowerment
Transformation Programming

*As you begin this section, you will already have mastered the
Self-Empowerment Alpha Ritual exercises. You should now be able to
sustain "Alpha level 25," a prerequisite for all self-programming.*

*The Mind/Body Feedback tests in Chapter 4, will give you a good
indication of your progress along the Alpha path.
I encourage you to try the Lemon Test — no matter what!*

"I AM"

Sharing My
Perfect Love Energy
With Everyone

CHAPTER 6

Preparing for Your Self-Transformation Program

Your Attitude

The importance of our attitudes, as we live alone and with others, cannot be overemphasized. In order to achieve positive biological and psychological changes, we must have a healthy, positive attitude. Because we all have different needs and different problems, each person's self-empowerment programming must be individualized. There are, however, certain fundamental needs we all share. Without a deep sense of *self-worth* and *perfect love* for ourselves and others, all efforts for self-improvement will be futile. Remember: *"Any good change that will come will come from the essence of perfect love energy."* Thus, a positive, loving, forgiving and benevolent attitude to ourselves and others must be the cornerstone of any self-empowerment program. Throughout many years of counseling, I have met women who could not be healed of illness. Many

God's Power is the result of Her *perfect love*. Transforming a life is the result of that same Power.

95

of these women had given up. They no longer cared for themselves or for others.

Radiation therapist, Dr. Carl Simonton, is a noted pioneer of positive thinking for cancer treatment. Simonton encourages his patients to love themselves and maintain a strong will to live. In many instances, he must teach them to change their attitudes about themselves. Simonton guides cancer patients to a new way of viewing not only themselves but *every aspect of their lives.* A spirit of hope and love for others and for self is fundamental to fighting disease. Simonton reports that the success of cancer treatment rises dramatically when patients are encouraged to think in terms of loving themselves and others.

Self-Appraisal

Before you create your individual self-empowerment program, you must establish your specific needs. Your first step is an honest "soul searching." Analyze yourself honestly. Appraise your behavior and look for those areas in which you are weak. Note the things you do which displease others. Consider the various moods you experience; think of your highs and lows. Think about your many physical needs; evaluate your body cycles and note any parts of your body that give you chronic discomfort. (Of course, if you have not already done so, you should first consult a physician about any serious physical disturbance.) After you have verified that a constant problem has to do with your negative thinking, *consider the effects of that problem.* Many of the discomforts we experience in our bodies are directly related to negative thought process.

After careful soul searching, begin thinking of how you would like to be. Draw a new mental image

Negative thinking is born of our sense of unworthiness.

of the person you want to become. See yourself be-having in a manner you find appealing. Begin feeling as you wish to feel. *When programming for any change, you must learn to generate the feelings which will accompany the change.* Remember that your image of *perfectly loving yourself* is critical to the success of your program. You are learning to see yourself from a new vantage point. As you reflect on your behavior, you will also see the potential for change. With Self-Empowerment Alpha Rituals you can teach yourself new habit patterns to become a happier, healthier person. The affirmations you create will be critical.

Language

Affirmations create impressions and impressions create thoughts. For example, if you hear the word "orange," you may think of a color or a fruit. If the reference is specific and you hear "Sunkist orange," your mind conjures up the fruit. Language is important because words not only convey information, *they act as powerful and remarkable stimuli.*

If you try the Lemon Test in Chapter 4, you will probably find that you salivate simply by thinking the word "lemon. " While you may not have a clear mental picture of a lemon itself, the word alone stimulates the sour taste, which makes you salivate. *The effect of words is a powerful world of cause and effect.* We are often not conscious of this. Imagine sitting in a room with a group of people and someone shivers, commenting, "It's cold!" Within moments, others will begin to feel that the room is chilly. *Suggestion itself creates results.* An excited, dynamic person can enliven a group of quiet, passive people by simply speaking enthusiastically.

Words affect our imaginations, thereby influencing our feelings. A single word may have many evocative associations. Consider the word "love." If someone tells you she loves you, your reaction will probably be warm and responsive. But if this same person were to say she disliked you, you would react defensively. Clearly, each word you choose to include in your personal set of program affirmations is important. It is essential that the meaning of all the language you select be clear to you.

Avoid the use of negative terminology. For instance, if you are creating a program to stop smoking, you would include an "I AM" affirmation such as, "I AM free from smoking," rather than "I do not smoke." "I avoid" is affirmative and active, without the negative "not." The mind doesn't register the "not." It is as if you are saying "I do smoke." The "not" is canceled out. Tell yourself you enjoy life without smoking. Put all statements into positive language. When negative words are used, the problem is only reinforced. If you are trying to alleviate pain, you will have better results with "my hand is numb and comfortable," than with "my hand is not hurting." The mind is influenced by main words: "comfortable" in the first example and "hurting" in the second. The word "hurting" alone, regardless of the fact that it is used with "not," will induce the mind to think of hurting. For this important reason, positive affirmations work most *effectively and should be used in all areas of self-improvement program design.*

The brain doesn't register the word "not."

Avoid the use of too many words in your affirmations. Say only what is necessary, and keep it brief. Always be certain that whatever you include is meaningful to you. Do not copy other people's words or ideas—use your own language because you will understand and respond to it easily.

When you use positive words, you can feel the power of your self-esteem.

98

Your Program and Your Daily Life

Keep in mind that, consciously or unconsciously, we receive information throughout our lives. We are *programmed* by many influences around us. Even during the time we are in the womb, we receive information, and when a baby is born, she has already received much external data. All the information we receive, externally or internally, plays itself out over the course of our lives. We are the culmination of our own thoughts and those from others.

Practice your Self-Empowerment Alpha Ritual exercises at least twice daily — once in the morning after you are fully awake, and again in the evening when you have finished your day's activities and before you become drowsy. A clear, relaxed mind retains affirmations better than one that is fighting off sleep or plagued by distracting thoughts. Affirmations for certain problems are most effective when repeated and practiced more than twice a day. Remember what Ag'nike said in Chapter One, "we are constantly *changing*. When you return to the village, it will be a different village. All the people will be different. Since it is true that we are always actively *changing*, it is also true that our *perfect love* energy, if we are not inspired to keep it active, will be left behind as we drift away. The waterfall energy drifts downstream and leaves the earth behind, does it not? The flame of the fire goes up in smoke and leaves us behind. If we leave our *perfect love* behind, Angelo, pain and suffering will follow. Each time you come to this place, separate yourself from the mundane issues in your world and repeat 'I am love' as I have told it to you. When you leave here, you will be a different person than when you came."

Changes are always occurring. You are the pilot who navigates your life's unfolding.

Ag'nike and her followers believed that their physical body could easily change from one moment to the next. Unlike the human consciousness which is infinite and unchangeable — the physical body can easily change from a wellness state to a sick state overnight. You can feel balanced and in harmony one moment and out of balance the next moment. Living *perfect love* was the source of their balanced energy. To remain balanced it was important to experience living *perfect love* on a daily basis.

As you and I already know, it is no secret, this philosophy of repeating positive thoughts and affirmations has been taught from the beginning of time and handed down through the many different religious and cult beliefs. We all need to be consistently reminded. Keep in mind that the success of your program depends largely on its consistent use. The more frequently you unite yourself to your affirmations, the sooner you will experience becoming your very thoughts. "Just as a women thinketh so is she."

101

"I AM"

"I AM" That "I AM"
is the
Very Core of My Being
There is No Other
Than "I AM"

CHAPTER

Self-Transformation Programs for Self-Confidence, Conquering Depression, Anxiety and Enjoying Natural Sleep

The Alpha rituals in this book can be used to transform negative emotions and attitudes into more positive ones. This chapter will focus on freedom from depression, freedom from anxiety, increasing self-confidence, and enjoying natural sleep.

Our habits and attitudes develop over a period of many years. We are the fruition of all our past experiences, positive and negative. Reversing the effects of these experiences takes place over time.

As you begin to use Self-empowerment Alpha Rituals, be patient with yourself. It may appear that little seems to happen at first. I assure you, when following Ag'nike's ancient wisdom, changes will happen. The slight changes you will learn to notice are feelings of greater relaxation and composure, and your attitude in general will become more positive.

The slightest indication of positive change is an improvement.

Begin with applying Alpha rituals to your minor problems. Bigger problems take a little longer to conquer; small ones allow you to progress more rapidly. Over time you will find yourself developing confidence in the use of these rituals, at which point you can move on to working on more significant changes.

Your behavior is most often consistent with how you feel about yourself. If you dislike yourself or are displeased with your behavior, the first thing you must do is adjust your self-image. Your self-image is the energizer for everything you think and do. "What you are," to yourself, either poisons or enhances your every action and thought.

The "I AM" as the "Self"

The "I AM" is your core self-image, your self-esteem; your connection to others and to God. It is your very spirit. "I AM" is significant because there is no other than "I AM." To search for answers in any other way sidesteps the core that generates everything in your world. You may hide your "I AM" from others, but it is still the essence of your very soul.

Loving yourself is having reverence for your "I AM."

To transform our lives, we must begin with the *perfect love* energy of the "I AM". "I AM" has power to create. The South American native women, through their *perfect love* waterfall ritual, learn the power of the "I AM" in their world. As they look into the stream beneath the waterfall and repeat aloud, "I AM love," they reinforce the power of their positive self-esteem — the power of what I have come to call the "I AM."

One morning as my partner Ken and I were unloading supplies from one of our large canoes, Ken groaned and muttered, "I'm feeling rotten." Omar, a native worker, perked up his ears and returned in broken English, "Just as you say, Master!" I turned to Piedad — "Please ask Ag'nike what Omar meant by that?" "Just as your friend said," Ag'nike answered. *"We believe that whatever you say of yourself is what you experience.* If you say, 'I am depressed,' then you will remain depressed until you say otherwise. If you say, 'I am poor,' you will remain so until you say otherwise. Our people believe that our whole life is what we believe of ourselves when we say 'I AM'."

Each of us has our unique daily life and therefore we believe we have special problems. But, in many respects, the problems we all have are very similar. The differences are particulars — people and circumstances. If you believe others have easier lives than you do, you are mistaken. Some people are in better control of their ups and downs; others hide their "I AM" so effectively that the rest of us cannot see the confusion they carry day and night.

You are the master of your own spirit, your own mind, and your own body. Let your "I AM" reflect that mastery. If you say, "I AM troubled," then you are creating and reflecting this truth. It is so. If you say, "I AM happy and content," then you are creating and reflecting this truth. It is so. "I AM" is your own creative truth. Figures 5 and 6, "I AM in my world," presents two views of yourself in relation to your world. The circles are your world; around your world are the problems you might encounter in your life. You stand in the center of this world.

The choice to change will only take a single thought.

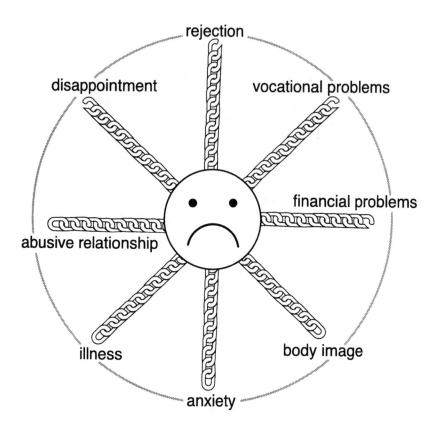

Figure 5 - My World <u>without</u> *Perfect Love* Energy
is Powerless!

In Figure 5, as you stand in the center of your world, you are controlled and made powerless by the problems in your life. Notice the chains, they link you to all your thoughts. You are bound by these chains — they influence you. Your thoughts are "I AM disappointed, I AM ill, I AM anxious, I AM financially poor, I AM without job. I AM in an abusive relationship, I AM being rejected." The natives would say, "Just as you say, master!" You have created the chains that control your thoughts. The chains have more power than you. You feel powerless to change the problems in your world.

106

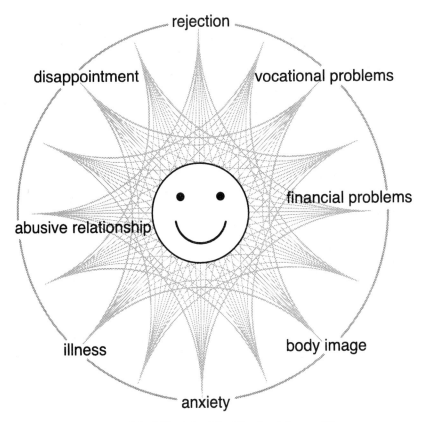

rejection

disappointment

vocational problems

financial problems

abusive relationship

illness

body image

anxiety

Figure 6 - My World <u>with</u> *Perfect Love* Energy
is Self-Empowered!

In Figure 6, you stand in the center of your world, empowered by the "I AM." You can cope with the many unpredictable aspects of life. You create beams of *perfect love* energy — they lead from you to your world. Because you feel clear, strong and confident, even in the face of chaos, you put forth *perfect love*. Your "I AM" does not allow discontent and fear to dominate and destroy your life.

Be mindful that problems and decisions are always part of our life. Even people in simple, primitive societies like the Rio Agua Clara villagers are not free from problems. They are constantly beset by failure and disappointment in all kinds of shapes and forms: men return to the village without food, fever plagues them, loved ones die. Every person on this earth is faced with the problem of survival. However, what I saw among these natives was that *perfect love* energy empowered them — they faced their traumas more easily than you or I.

As a self-empowered woman in *perfect love* energy, you can take on the changes of life, both good and bad. As you respect and utilize the unlimited strength of your "I AM," life becomes less discouraging and flows more easily. Your Self-Empowerment Alpha Ritual is your authority for your "I AM" transformation.

When you respect yourself, you acknowledge your power.

CREATING YOUR OWN POSITIVE EMOTIONS

Self-Transformation for Freedom from Depression

Depression is one of the most common emotional problems in our society. Women and men in all walks of life suffer from it. An endless variety of medicines are sold over the counter and by prescription to help people who struggle with depression. In our busy world, we have forgotten about staying centered. "I AM" is the reinforcement of your center.

I encourage my clients who suffer from depression to avoid even thinking of the word. Instead of telling people how depressed you are, start saying to yourself, "I am content and hopeful." Like some organic diseases, I have always thought depression to be contagious. I will never forget a sight that seemed to be a striking proof of this: During my ministerial days, preaching one Sunday morning from the pulpit, I observed in the congregation three unrelated women who

A positive and immediate cure for depression: bake a cake and give it to a neighbor.

were seeing me privately and individually for depression counseling. They were all sitting together! Unknowingly, they had surrounded themselves with depressed energy. Seek out as much positive energy as you can. Use the following "I AM" affirmations in your Alpha ritual for freedom from depression, or you may create your own.

Your Self-Limiting Beliefs About Depression

The following self-limiting beliefs list will help you identify problem areas for perfect love self-transformation. Go down the list honestly. Do not consider the opinions of others. If you keep in mind that you love yourself, you will realize that the self-limiting beliefs involve no right or wrong, good or bad. They are simply you. In perfect love, we withhold judgment. Which are the self-limiting beliefs you would like to change?

Self-Limiting Beliefs List

1. I experience feelings of depression often.
2. I am more critical of myself than is necessary.
3. I experience feelings of insecurity.
4. I do not like myself.
5. I have difficulty coping with situations I cannot control.
6. I feel powerless to change.
7. I consider myself nervous and high-strung.
8. I feel unfairly treated by others.
9. My feelings of tension increase in certain situations.
10. I worry more than I should.

Now, that you have completed reading this list, how do you really, deep inside, feel about some of them? Take a moment to honestly connect with your feelings.

Now ask yourself: Are there any you would like to remove from your belief system? Would you like to change any of them? Next, select from the following list of "I AM" affirmations—those that make you feel empowered.

"I AM" Affirmations for Freedom from Depression

Through the years, I have used many of these same affirmations with my clients. Nearly all the women I have counseled were able to achieve their self-improvement goals. Carefully contemplate these sample affirmations and select the ones you feel would help you achieve your *perfect love* self-empowerment goals.

1. I AM God's beautiful love energy.
2. I AM the master of my spirit, mind and body.
3. I AM free from worry each and every day.
4. I AM manifesting *perfect love* energy.
5. I AM sharing my love freely with others.
6. I AM free of my depression.
7. I AM an optimistic and positive thinker.
8. I AM in God's perfect will.
9. I AM accepting my womanhood completely.
10. I AM hopeful and enthusiastic about my life.

Suggestion: *You may want to post your selected "I AM" affirmations on your bathroom mirror or some other place where you will see them regularly.*

Self-Transformation for Freedom from Anxiety

Fear always invites more fear and more fear creates phobias.

We all experience fear under certain real-life conditions. Fear is a defense signal that tells us when to protect ourselves. Fear is normal and healthy when there is truly something to fear such as an intruder in your house or an attack by a mountain lion while camping.

For some of us, however, fears become exaggerated, irrational and unfounded. These fears, amplified as they are to unrealistic levels, are known as *phobias*.

Most people are mildly phobic in some way. Others are extremely phobic — their fears dominate their lives. The phobia usually begins with a past negative experience. Instead of diminishing with time, fear of the negative experience increases until it is no longer realistic. For example, a child may fall out of her crib. Gradually, her fear of high places becomes so extreme that as an adult she is afraid to climb stairs, cross bridges, or look out of windows. The original incident has long been forgotten; now the mind is conditioned to be fearful, even when it has no reason to be.

Case History: At the time I was director of the Humantics Health Centers in Los Angeles in 1988, a new client who was beginning our program for alcohol addiction had made her first appointment to see me. I waited in my office for her, but she did not show up. Looking up her number, I called to find out what had happened. She hesitated to explain, and then finally blurted out, "I did come to your office at 10 o'clock this morning. But I was afraid to use the elevator or stairs, which have an open outside balcony! I'm afraid of heights, and if your office was on the ground floor I could have made my appointment."

It is a good idea to have someone help you through the transformation.

I suggested she meet me at the bottom of the stairs and I would guide her past the open balcony. She agreed. We began her Self-Empowerment Ritual program for her phobia as part of her treatment. After two weeks of practice, she was able to climb the stairs without any assistance. Five weeks later, she began using the elevator. She shared with me that in the past, the only way she could get past her fears on a daily basis was by drinking. Once her fears were removed, she was able to conquer her alcohol problem.

Your Self-Limiting Beliefs

The following self-limiting beliefs will help you identify problem areas for *perfect love* self-transformation. Go down the list honestly. Do not consider the opinions of others. If you keep in mind that you love yourself, you will realize that the self-limiting beliefs involve no right or wrong, good or bad. They are simply you. In *perfect love*, we withhold our judgment.

Self-Limiting Beliefs List

1. I am always concerned about unimportant things.
2. I do not understand why I have certain fears.
3. Some of my fears are not rational.
4. I have difficulty trusting people.
5. I repeat certain actions compulsively.
6. I feel I am a failure.
7. I do few things well.
8. I over-analyze everything.
9. I feel very insecure.
10. I have difficulty making decisions.

Now, that you have completed reading this list, how do you really deep inside feel about some of them? Take a moment to honestly connect with your feelings.

Self-evaluation is often difficult and always revealing.

Now ask yourself: Are there any you would like to remove from your belief system? Would you like to change any of them? Next, select from the following list of "I AM" affirmations those that make you feel empowered.

"I AM" Affirmations for Freedom from Anxiety

Carefully contemplate these sample affirmations and select the ones you feel will help you achieve your *perfect love* self-empowerment for freedom from anxiety, or you can create your own.

1. I AM *perfect love* energy.
2. I AM a rational woman.
3. I AM an empowered woman.
4. I AM secure in my feelings.
5. I AM free from my past negative influences.
6. I AM a courageous woman.
7. I AM always replacing fear with love.
8. I AM loving myself perfectly.
9. I AM in control of my feelings.
10. I AM the master of my spirit, mind and body.

Suggestion: *You may want to post your selected "I AM" affirmations on your bathroom mirror or some other place where you will see them regularly.*

Self-Transformation for Increasing Self-Confidence

Everyone begins life with some degree of self-confidence. Think of young children. Most of them do not hesitate to play with other children. They would rather be in the company of others than be alone. They have a healthy sense of confidence.

Unfortunately, throughout our lives, incidents occur that diminish our self-confidence. We begin to have feelings of worthlessness that becomes difficult to shake off. Each failure reinforces subsequent failure, and we become programmed with self-taught low self-esteem.

You may be a person who has created a "failure syndrome" for herself. Imagine a child learning to walk. As she learns, she will fall again and again. If she were to take these repeated failures to heart rather than continue instinctively to keep trying to walk, she would never progress beyond crawling. Thus, it is in our very instinct to ignore failure and keep pushing ahead. Some people have been so discouraged early in life that they no longer strive for success. The important thing to remember is that there is always good reason to believe in our success. It is important to recognize those factors we cannot control and do our best to change the ones we can. Nothing is ever all bad.

This very moment is your new beginning.

A major problem for those with low self-confidence is being afraid to communicate with others. For example, you may remain silent in a class discussion rather than participate and share your thoughts. You may want to speak up, but the very idea of joining the discussion makes you become anxious, nervous and inhibited. These feelings make you withdraw even more. You reach the point that your doubt stops you in your tracks. You live in a tiny world you have created within your doubts and fears.

Your Self-Limiting Beliefs

The following self-limiting beliefs will help you identify problem areas for *perfect love* self-transformation. Go down the list honestly. Do not consider the opinions of others. If you keep in mind that you love yourself, you will realize that the self-limiting beliefs involve no right or wrong, good or bad. They are simply you. In *perfect love*, we withhold our judgment.

114

Self-Limiting Beliefs List

1. I have trouble feeling comfortable with people.
2. I think most people are better than I am.
3. I seldom do anything right.
4. I am an introvert.
5. I do not like people very much.
6. I do not like myself.
7. I feel different from most people.
8. I am unsure of my self.
9. I do not complete many projects that I begin.
10. I dwell on my past failures.

Now, that you have completed reading this list, how do you really deep inside feel about some of them? Take a moment to honestly connect with your feelings.

Now ask yourself: Are there any you would like to remove from your belief system? Would you like to change any of them? Next, select from the following list of "I AM" affirmations those that make you feel empowered.

Self-judgement without love is harmful.

"I AM" Affirmations for Increasing Self-Confidence

Carefully contemplate these sample affirmations and select the ones you feel will help you achieve your *perfect love* self-empowerment for Increasing Self-Confidence, or you can create your own.

1. I AM able to make decisions.
2. I AM comfortable around people I used to think were superior to me.
3. I AM loving myself perfectly.
4. I AM liked by most people.
5. I AM feeling good about myself.
6. I AM an intelligent woman.
7. I AM a successful woman.
8. I AM comfortable around the opposite sex.
9. I AM able to do many things very well.
10. I AM able to express myself easily and clearly.

Suggestion: *You may want to post your selected "I AM" affirmations on your bathroom mirror or some other place where you will see them regularly.*

Case History: Barbara, a 30-year-old computer programmer, had been raised by an authoritarian, perfectionist father. Nothing Barbara did as a child was right, and even what she did as an adult displeased him. Barbara's self-esteem was abysmally low and became even worse when her husband of four years filed for divorce and left her. Barbara plunged into a deep depression. She was afraid she would now lose her job. Overweight, filled with despair and climbing deeper into negativity, she found herself growing terrified of men.

In therapy, Barbara sobbed and told me she did nothing well — everyone in the world was more capable than she. On the list of self-limiting beliefs above, she felt she could circle every one. With a bit of encouragement from me, Barbara reluctantly created a list of affirmations. As I took her through a Basic Relaxation Ritual, she was able to accept the idea of listening to the affirmations I read off to her. I suggested she record them on a tape for herself, but she declined — the sound of her own voice repeating positive words

Barbara had discovered her beauty within.

116

was too much for her. I suggested she ask a friend to speak onto the tape. She said she would try.

A week later, Barbara had a tape ready. In addition, using visualization and mental theater, she worked on two scenarios: seeing herself in an office setting as a busy and well-liked computer programmer, and chatting at a party with a man. As Barbara practiced self-empowerment rituals with her tape and mental-theater exercises, she began to feel better about herself. She told me she was very surprised. I encouraged her to stick with the rituals and see what happened. In five months, Barbara reported much more confidence at work; even her co-workers had commented on a change in her and she was put in charge of a new project. In the realm of dating, Barbara had gone out to dinner with a couple of men who lived in her apartment complex and she had greatly enjoyed the evenings. "I never thought anyone would want to sit across a table from me or want to spend money on me in any way. Both these men were so nice — there was no pressure of any kind. They just told me they enjoyed being with me and wanted to see me have a good time. I feel so relieved."

Self-Transformation for Unhealthy Sleep Habits

The key to natural sleep is accepting sleep as a normal, necessary body function. You do not *try* to sleep. You learn to relax and surrender to sleep. Anticipate sleep and enjoy it. The harder you try to fall asleep, the more awake you will become. Sleep comes with relaxation. People who have difficulty entering a natural sleep state usually go to bed with active minds; they often worry about their problems just before sleep. An active mind will often interfere with natural sleep.

117

As a child you were told to "go to sleep." Now there is only you "allowing sleep."

If you have been relying on sleep-inducing aids, you must program your mind to accept sleep as a natural phenomenon in order to break your dependency on these compounds. When you believe that you are able to sleep by relaxing and letting go of all concerns, you will free yourself from tension and anxiety.

Poor sleep habits may mean that you cannot easily fall asleep and/or that you wake up during the night and remain awake. Your sleeping-and-waking syndrome may be repeated several times a night.

Your Self-Limiting Beliefs About Your Sleep

The following self-limiting beliefs will help you identify problem areas for *perfect love* self-transformation. Go down the list honestly. Do not consider the opinions of others. If you keep in mind that you love yourself, you will realize that the self-limiting beliefs involve no right or wrong, good or bad. They are simply you. In *perfect love*, we withhold our judgment.

Self-limiting Beliefs

1. I have difficulty falling asleep.
2. I wake up after I have slept only for a little while.
3. I depend on pills to sleep.
4. I have nightmares.
5. I think of my problems as I try to fall asleep.
6. My sleep is interrupted by sounds around me.
7. I associate sleep with death.
8. I am afraid of the dark.
9. I am afraid of falling asleep and not waking up.
10. I sleep badly and don't feel rested when I wake up.

"I AM" Affirmations for Enjoying Natural Sleep

Carefully contemplate these sample affirmations and select the ones you feel will help you achieve your *perfect love* self-empowerment for Enjoying Natural Sleep, or you can create your own.

Before retiring, say to yourself: "I AM in God's Perfect Will."

1. I AM able to sleep naturally.
2. I AM accepting sleep as natural and safe.
3. I AM accepting sleep like other healthy people.
4. I AM allowing harmless sounds in my environment to help me sleep.
5. I AM capable of sleeping peacefully and having pleasant dreams.
6. I AM capable of sleeping without interruption tonight.
7. I AM taking loving thoughts to bed with me.
8. I AM able to easily accept sleep whenever I choose.
9. I AM no longer trying to fall asleep, I simply accept sleep.
10. I AM free from past negatives which have interfered with my restful sleep.

Suggestion: *You may want to post your selected "I AM" affirmations on your bathroom mirror, or some other place where you will see them regularly.*

Case History: Mona, 42, was the wife of a busy attorney whose practice kept him at his office late into the night several times a week. Then Mona, a concert pianist, would eat dinner alone with her three children. On the nights Mona performed, the children would stay with their aunt. Mona came to see me for her insomnia. She had suffered from it for seven years, tossing and turning unless she got up and took the pills her doctor had prescribed. For a time, Mona took the pills every night, but with constant use, they had become less and less effective. Desperate, Mona began drinking a large jug of white wine every night to relax and sleep. This made her problem worse. She became almost non-functional, unable to care for her children or perform as a pianist.

I asked Mona which of the self-limiting beliefs applied to her. She had circled "I have nightmares" and "I think of my problems as I try to fall asleep." We talked about her nightmares, one of which was very striking: She would be performing under the lights in a concert hall and she would notice her children sitting in the audience with strangers. Then she would notice tears and fear on her children's faces. She would want to get up from the piano, but in the dream she could not. She played faster and faster, the piano keeping her prisoner. Her children would scream out for her from the audience seats. Still Mona could not stop playing and get up. The music got louder and louder until Mona would awaken, bathed in sweat.

I suggested that Mona felt guilty that her children did not have enough attention from either herself or her husband. She agreed. She said she did not know how to explain to her husband that his practice was ruining his family life. She felt she should give up her music and concert performing to make it up to her children. But the thought of that made her feel terrible—her creativity and true expression of herself came through her music. Until she became pregnant, it had been the most important thing in her life. Mona's husband had been attracted to her for that part of her identity initially. To give it up would be a mistake.

Mona began to practice self-empowerment in the Alpha rituals I taught her. She repeated a list of affirmations for self-love to give herself the strength

Our dreams are often a clue to our subconscious thoughts.

to approach her husband to re-evaluate their priorities. As Mona grew more positive, she noticed what she called a "ripple effect." Her husband grew less frenetic about his work. Their relationship improved and Mona seized the opportunity to broach the subject of quality of family life. To her surprise, he showed enormous cooperation and relief. "I've been pulled in the wrong direction," he told Mona. "It's time to pull myself back."

In tandem with her self-love affirmations, Mona repeated affirmations to allow herself to relax at night and sleep without her pills. Gradually, they began to work. "I'm beginning to see how this is all knitted together," said Mona. "It wasn't a matter of my sleeping problem alone. I had to find what lay beneath that. Practicing *perfect love* for myself — the way I practice my piano every day — was the key. It began to undo the negativity. And, since I know I have to keep practicing piano for the rest of my life, I'll know to also practice my *perfect love*! How could I forget?"

As you create your affirmations, choose those that particularly apply to you. If you are a light sleeper and are constantly waken by sounds at night, program yourself to think of these as cue sounds that help you sleep. If you did not have a sleeping problem at any time in the past, use an affirmation to remind yourself that you are capable of healthful sleeping now, as you did before. Remember that many sleep disorders stem from issues that are eating away at you. When, like Mona, you can identify these issues, self-empowerment, self-love and a little time and effort, will make a significant difference. You will be surprised at how much more easily deep and fulfilling rest will come to you at night.

To sleep peacefully, you can interpret your environmental sounds as cues.

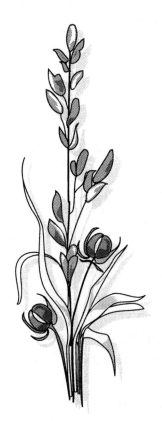

"I AM"

Able to Communicate
Easily and Clearly
with Everyone

CHAPTER

Your Sexual Love Life and Body Image

SECTION "A"

Self-Transformation for Sex Problems

Sex without *perfect love* is usually limited. A sexual experience without love can be painful and crippling. The sex act should be the shared climax of two individuals growing together and becoming one in a transcendence of themselves. If you have had any problems achieving regular and gratifying sex with a partner you love, you know how true this is. Realizing that sexual gratification is a gateway to energy, not only in a physical sense but also in a spiritual and psychic sense, you know the importance of sexual fulfillment.

The ultimate sexual high is the complementary orgasm each shares with the other.

Perfect Love Sexual Response

As you begin any program to correct sexual difficulties, you should recognize the essentials of a healthy, satisfying, mutually fulfilling sexual exchange. The most meaningful relationships grow from couples joined in union because of their love for one another. The understanding and sensitivity of one human being for another is a prerequisite for any gratifying shared experience.

Women today are conscious of their mind, body and spirit as part of sexual experience. The fact remains that this "wholeness" of experience is ideal; the inhibitions most of us carry to some degree make it more of a wish or dream. There is no question that a woman's sexuality is complex. *Perfect love*, while not practiced by many, can be a major boon to sexual fulfillment with a partner. Your entire relationship with your mate affects your sexual activity as a couple. Living in *perfect love* energy will help both of you tremendously, as the energy you give out is what you receive. *"Any good change that will come will come from the essence of your perfect love energy."*

Expect and receive the love and respect you deserve from your partner.

Improving Sexual Harmony with Your Partner

Although the following questions are not sexual issues in and of themselves, decide which ones apply to you.

1. Do you feel you contribute more to your relationship than your partner?
2. Does he/she make you feel sexually unattractive?
3. Is he/she less attractive to you now than he/she was in the past?
4. Do you have doubt as to your attractiveness to your partner?

5. Is your sexual desire greater than your partner's, thereby causing you sexual frustration?
6. Do you feel sex in your relationship has become routine and boring?
7. Does your partner behave in a passive way?
8. Does your partner behave like he/she is in a hurry to get sex over and done with?
9. Is your partner insensitive and not romantic to you during sex?
10. Do you and your partner have conflicting needs and expectations where sex is concerned?
11. Do you often think of having sex with someone other than your partner?
12. Are/were you sexually inhibited with your present or former partner(s)?

If you answered "yes" to any of these questions, you and your partner should have a serious talk. Often these problems can be overcome through honest communication. Partners are frequently unaware of their sexual shortcomings, particularly if the women they are with tolerate a problem silently without talking about it. No one wants to admit they cannot sexually satisfy their partner.

Sexual fulfillment with a partner is the manifestation of *perfect love* in its most ecstatic form. Through sex, two people move completely into one another and share the enormous pleasure of physical and spiritual climax. Sexual climax is most satisfying when both partners pass beyond conscious awareness of themselves and their environment, fusing shared desires, sensations and emotions as they experience *perfect love* together. Both partners pass beyond conscious awareness of themselves and their environment, as they experience *perfect love* together. The living *perfect love* Self-

There are no bad sexual experiences, only bad communications.

125

Empowerment Alpha Ritual is your key for producing pleasurable and satisfying sexual response.

The following questions will help you identify problem areas which you may want to address in your self-empowerment transformation goals. Go through the list honestly. Do not consider the opinions of others. Remember, there are no right or wrong choices. Consider the ones you would like to change.

1. Do you sometimes fail to have an orgasm during sexual intercourse?
2. Do you have difficulty lubricating (vaginally) during sexual intercourse?
3. Is it difficult for you to reach orgasm when masturbating?
4. Do you fail to reach orgasm when your partner stimulates you (manually)?
5. When you near the point of orgasm, do you try to force yourself to orgasm?
6. Do you have difficulty reaching orgasm during oral sex?
7. Do you think of yourself as sexually unattractive?
8. Do you have difficulty getting sexually aroused?
9. Do you experience vaginal discomfort or pain with penetration?
10. Are you embarrassed to be naked with your partner?
11. Have you been sexually abused as a child or adult?
12. Are you holding anger or resentment against your abusers?
13. Do you carry guilt from your past sexual experiences?
14. Have you been betrayed and violated by a family member?

Now, that you have completed reading these questions, how do you feel about some of them? Take time to honestly connect with your feelings.

Ask yourself: Are there any you would like to change or remove. Next, select from the following list of affirmations those that make you feel empowered.

"I AM" Affirmations for Sexual Harmony

Through the years, I have used many of these same affirmations with my clients. Nearly all the women I have counseled were able to achieve their self-improvement goals. Carefully contemplate these sample affirmations and select the ones you feel would help you achieve your *perfect love* self-empowerment goals.

1. I AM *perfect love* energy.
2. I AM the master of my spirit, mind and body.
3. I AM a normal, sexually functioning female.
4. I AM able to relax and enjoy vaginal penetration.
5. I AM able to accept and enjoy orgasm.
6. I AM able to relax and accept my sex partner.
7. I AM allowing myself to reach orgasm without trying so hard.
8. I AM enjoying sex without tension and anxiety.
9. I AM aware that making love is a beautiful, satisfying experience.
10. I AM free from all my past sexual fears.

Suggestion: *You may want to post your selected "I AM" affirmations on your bathroom mirror or some other place where you will see them regularly.*

If you find any of the above affirmations embarrassing or disturbing, your problem may be that you are embarrassed by sex. Women raised in a strict religious environment often learn early that sex is unmen-

Romance will enhance your harmonious sexual orgasm.

127

tionable and a necessary evil. Negative sexual conditioning is bound to produce sexual inhibition and frustration, not to mention guilt and fear. If even discussing sex is forbidden, what can you expect of sex itself?

Case History: Diane's First Orgasm During Sex

Diane, 31, had been married seven years when she saw me for therapy. She complained she had never experienced orgasm while having sex with her husband. However, she sometimes had an orgasm during oral sex with her husband or when she masturbated. On the list of questions I handed Diane (see questions above), she answered "yes" to the question about vaginal discomfort during sex. We discussed how she felt about her husband's penis and penises in general. Diane was embarrassed to engage in the discussion, but eventually confessed that she was frightened of penetration. As a result, when faced with the prospect of intercourse, she became nervous, anxious, and her vagina became dry.

Diane agreed to practice self-transformation rituals for sexual harmony. Because she was unwilling to discuss why exactly she had such a reaction to the male organ, I suggested she create a list of positive affirmations she could accept and use. After several weeks of practice in private, Diane found herself feeling more relaxed and comfortable with her husband. During sex, she was able to remain at ease. She did not try to force herself to climax; she allowed herself to relax and enjoy the act of sex. Two months into her Alpha rituals, Diane experienced her first orgasm with her husband. From that time on, she was able to relax and enjoy the normal, pleasant experience of shared sexual fulfillment.

Healing Childhood Sexual Abuse

Many women have experienced sexual abuse in their lives, the saddest of which occurs in childhood. It is no wonder that so many women in our world are sexually confused, frightened and angry. Recovery from such victimization can take a lifetime, particularly if women who have had these experiences keep silent and tell no one. Luckily, your self-transformation Alpha rituals are completely private, and I encourage you to be open and to broach the subject of sexual abuse in your healing exercises.

The affirmations below, practiced with the philosophy of living *perfect love*, do help. I have seen their effect on the women I have professionally and personally counseled. The first requirement — almost a covenant — is to begin to believe that you are the most important person in all the universe. Yes, YOU! You must begin to believe this. You must begin to love yourself perfectly because you deserve it. Each one of you must commit to this truth. Ag'nike and the Rio Agua Clara women believed in their individual conscious selves — as they glanced at their reflections in the stream at the foot of the gorgeous waterfall, they knew what they were looking at was the most important person in the universe. The daily waterfall ritual was to remind them of this, and to remind them of the love they deserved while they lived on the earth. You, too, deserve that love.

Accepting the "I AM" spirit, is believing in your importance.

No one can take your importance away from you. It is your "I AM" birthright. Move away from your past, and you can make things different in your life today. Your spirit, mind and body have unlimited potential for producing change. When you were a toddler learning to walk, the first time you tumbled, what

"It is always my choice to transform my life."

129

did you do? You looked surprised, got up and tried again. As a little girl, learning to ride a bicycle, the first time you fell off it, what did you do? You got back on and peddled again. How many times did you fall while trying to walk? *If you took each fall to heart, feeling dreadful failure, you would not be walking today.* You would have never gotten past your negative programming. But today, you walk, talk, skate, ride a bike, drive a car, use a computer, and on and on. You were not held back by the times you failed when you were learning these things.

Remember, you can always create a perfect moment.

Without even thinking about it, we are always making decisions and changes in our lives for good and bad. Sometimes we choose a path because our negative programming dominates in the decision; other times, our positive programming tells us what to do.

Living *perfect love* is a positive inner world you can enter into whenever you choose to do so. Each time you feel it, you heal. That is its power. It cannot take away your past, but it can help you regain the essence of yourself that was stolen from you as a child, and perhaps later as an adult again. Living *perfect love* and Alpha self-empowerment can help you produce pleasurable and satisfying sexual response, no matter what has happened before. Just remember! Ag'nike and her little tribe of followers lived in the present moment by consistently loving themselves. Today is the beginning of the rest of your life. Recently, Louise Hay handed me a card that she pass out to her friends. I want to share it with you now. Remember the following whenever you are having a problem, *"All is well. Everything is working out for my highest good. Out of this situation only good will come. I am safe!"*

130

Affirmations to Heal Childhood Sexual Abuse

Select the affirmations that are relevant for you and use as many as you like. You may also want to choose some from the first part of this Chapter 8. Most of these affirmations have helped many women like you.

Sexual freedom emanates from accepting your sexual feelings, "I AM OK."

1. I AM free from all the damage of my past sexual abuse.
2. I AM innocent of my childhood sexual abuse.
3. I AM accepting my sexual feelings free of guilt.
4. I AM blessed by God to freely enjoy my sexual desires.
5. I AM empowered to freely express my sexual feelings.
6. I AM accepting the right to experience my sexual feelings.
7. I AM now living and enjoying my female sexual feelings.
8. I AM blameless for my childhood sexual abuse.
9. I AM guiltless of my childhood sexual actions.
10. I AM free of all remorse and shame from my childhood sexual display.

Now, that you have completed reading these ten affirmations, how do you feel about some of them? Take a moment to honestly connect with your feelings

Now ask yourself: Are there any you would like to change or remove. Next, select the "I AM" affirmations that make you feel the change would be an improvement.

Suggestion: *You may want to post your selected "I AM" affirmations on your bathroom mirror or some other place where you will see them regularly.*

SECTION "B"

Self-Transformation for Your New Body Image

People are more overweight as a population than they have ever been. Weight problems are shared by young and old, rich and poor throughout the nation. If we were all to realize that "Any good change that will come will come from the essence of your *perfect love* energy," we would be able to create the self-empowerment to control this and other aspects of our lives.

As you become master of your spirit, you become master of your mind and body. Before you begin your Self-Empowerment Alpha Ritual weight-control program, make a list of the reasons you want to lose weight. (For instance: You deserve the pleasure of a healthy and beautiful body. You deserve to enjoy your favorite physical activities.) Remind yourself of your motivation. If one of your reasons is to improve your appearance, remind yourself of the clothes you will be wearing when you reach your weight goal. Begin to think of yourself as looking attractive now.

Begin each morning by acknowledging the beautiful you within.

Setting Your Weight Goal

Be realistic about your desired weight. Consider the size of your body frame. Are you small or large? How much did you weigh 10, 15, 20 years ago? Track your weight pattern over the years. Many women set unrealistic goals — for instance, to weigh what they did at age 18 or 25. You may not be able to comfortably slide back to this weight, as it is normal for most of us to gain a few extra pounds as we age.

Set short-term goals. Think of your weight loss in ounces rather than pounds. (Remember, you gained your extra weight by ounces!) Lasting, effective weight loss is slow and regular. Be patient. Give yourself a week to 10 days to reach your first weight goal. Stick to this time frame for each new goal. Do not try to lose more than two pounds per week. Crash dieting is harmful to your body and the weight you lose is rarely permanent.

If you lose an ounce a day, you will lose seven ounces a week (almost half a pound), and at this conservative pace you will drop 25 pounds in one year. This is a comfortable rate of loss that allows you to make your new health habits (such as eating less and exercising more) a part of your life-style. With discipline and perseverance you can make the necessary changes to achieve a satisfying and healthy weight.

Overeating is frequently the result of tension. For example, one day you decide to wear an outfit you haven't warn for sometime, shocked by the fact it is way too tight, you hurry to weigh yourself on your bathroom scale, screaming — "it can't be!" The scale registers 7 pounds more than your normal weight. You become frustrated which causes tension which then acts as a stimulus for overeating. The uncontrolled eating results in weight increase. The problem is a vicious circle, as illustrated in Figure 7, next page.

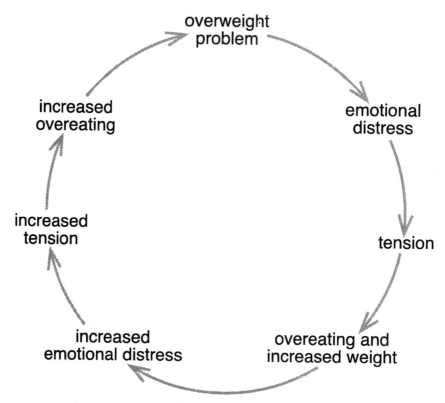

Figure 7 - Overeating Behavior Cycle

Overeating Behavior Cycle

If you experience this overeating behavior cycle, you can relieve your tension problem by always including the following "I AM" affirmations: 13. "I AM in control of my emotions" and 14. "I AM convinced of my self-empowerment to control my weight."

Ask yourself the following questions to help you identify specifics in your eating habits. Be honest and truthful with your answers.

You can easily break the "cycle" with self-love.

134

1. Do you eat more than you should when you are alone?
2. Do you eat right before going to bed?
3. Do you eat candy and other sweets to excess?
4. Do you use too much margarine, butter and other fats?
5. Do you habitually snack between meals?
6. Do you eat until you are very full?
7. Do you overeat when you are frustrated?
8. Do your extra calories come from alcohol?
9. Do you think of yourself as fat?
10. Do you dislike yourself?
11. Are you sexually frustrated?
12. Do you avoid physical exercise?
13. Do you eat your meals and snacks too quickly?
14. Do you resolve to "eat less tomorrow" to make up for today?
15. Do you eat standing up?

Now, that you have completed reading the above questions, how do you feel about some of them? Take a moment to honestly connect with your feelings

Now ask yourself: Are there any you would like to remove from daily life? Would you like to change any of them? Next, select from the following list of "I AM" affirmations those that make you feel empowered and confident.

Self-Transformation Affirmations for Weight Control

Through the years, I have used many of these same affirmations with my clients. Nearly all the women I have counseled were able to achieve their self-improvement goals. Carefully contemplate these sample affirmations and select the ones you feel will help you achieve your *perfect love* self-empowerment goals.

1. I AM *perfect love* energy.
2. I AM the master of my mind, spirit and body.
3. I AM avoiding snacks between meals.
4. I AM enjoying chewing my food slowly.
5. I AM avoiding high-fat foods.
6. I AM avoiding sweets and sugar.
7. I AM no longer eating standing up.
8. I AM able to visualize the new, thin me.
9. I AM eating smaller portions of food.
10. I AM no longer needing food as my "fix."
11. I AM healthy and loving myself.
12. I AM consistent with my weight program.
13. I AM in control of my emotions.
14. I AM convinced of my self-empowerment to control my weight.
15. I AM enjoying daily exercises.
16. I AM fulfilling myself sexually.
17. I AM allowing myself to relax free of alcohol.
18. I AM enjoying my own company.
19. I AM able to sleep comfortably without more food.

Remember, you are always changing and becoming the "beautiful you."

Suggestion: *You may want to post your selected "I AM" affirmations on your bathroom mirror or some other place where you will see them regularly.*

Case History: Carol Loses Weight with Self-Love

Carol, 33, was a single mother who weighed 168 pounds when she came to me. She ate constantly between meals, snacking several times a day. She usually ate much more than she needed to feel full. She rarely did any physical exercise. She had low self-esteem and did not have positive feelings about herself. For three years Carol had tried different diets without success.

After four sessions of repeating "I AM" affirmations while in Alpha, Carol tuned into her higher consciousness and began to feel real love for herself. Self-empowered, she pulled out of her depression and her confidence to succeed became much higher. By giving herself the chance to love herself completely, she created a new self-image. She imagined herself learning to manage her eating habits. She pictured herself at mealtimes eating only those foods that brought her good health. She imagined the way she looked and the clothes she would wear at the weight she wanted to achieve. She recalled how she had looked when she was thin. She imagined herself on a scale that weighed her at 125 pounds (her goal). After 10 months, Carol was down to 125 pounds. She had lost 34 pounds — about 13 ounces each week — a little less then one pound a week.

Keep your "will" and your new self-image in agreement, and you will succeed.

"I AM"

Consciously Aware
of My Own
Perfect Love Energy
and
God's Unlimited
Power in Me

CHAPTER

The Power of Perfect Love to Conquer Addiction

I have realized from living my own life and counseling others for help with their addiction that *whenever we want something too much, it will eventually make us powerless.* Today, we live in a society driven by marketing, and the lust for material goods has already taken millions of us into deep financial waters. We continue to be slaves to our desires, not all of which are for "things." Some desires are for substances such as alcohol or drugs that alter the way we feel. Some of us are able to indulge in these substances recreationally, without *wanting it too much* and remaining empowered, but others of us are not able to exercise enough control to keep pleasure-seeking to a moderate level. We want it too much, as a result we find ourselves powerless.

Your empowerment begins with your self-love.

An addiction is different from a habit because it is both a physical and psychological compulsion which must be satisfied. A physical addiction results from the body's repeated desire for a substance; a psychologi-

139

cal addiction is the mind's repeated desire for an experience. Addicts are slaves to their physical and psychological needs.

After many years of helping people become free of their addictions, I have concluded that there is usually an underlying reason for these compulsions. The reason is usually rooted in fear of accepting *perfect love* from the self (the "I AM") and others, which causes feelings of low self-confidence, low self-esteem and low self-worth. We reach into our infancy to replicate those safe situations that gave us warmth and security in a threatening world.

As adults, we re-create oral pacification — the safe, happy feeling a baby gets from nursing at her mother's breast — by way of oral pacification: smoking, eating, drinking, and even chewing gum or tobacco. Sucking a nipple is replaced with sucking on a cigarette, and is connected with the security of being held and nursed and loved. *Addicts are looking for self-confidence, security and love.* Unfortunately, no cigarette, candy bar or shot of vodka can really give us these things. Many of us enter the self-destructive path of overuse and self-abuse, only making our existence worse. Remember, *whenever we want something too much, it will eventually make us powerless.* First we deny our self-love, then our self-esteem, then our self-confidence and finally our self-empowerment. Yes, we really feel powerless.

The first step to regain our self-empowerment is to acknowledge our right to deserve *perfect love* from ourselves and others. The self-transformation programs in this section will help you re-program your mind and regain your self-empowerment. As long as you have been satisfying your particular addiction, you have been *reinforcing it.* An alcoholic renews her drinking compulsion each time she has a drink. A smoker

Loving yourself frees your need for oral pacification.

140

fortifies her addiction with each cigarette she smokes. The addicted eater reinforces her poor eating habits every time she overindulges herself with food. Repeating any habit over and over makes it part of memory and behavior. Because of their power over the mind and body addictions not easy to overcome.

You can increase your ritual sessions to two or three a day. The more often your affirmations are able to work on your addiction-programmed memory, the more quickly you will notice results. Time and perseverance are the key.

Horace Mann, (American educator 1800s) compared a habit pattern to a cable: We weave a thread of this cable each day until finally it is not possible to break. An addiction, like a cable, is reinforced by repetition until it is too strong to break with will power alone.

My years of treating clients with addictions have shown that once you are able to acknowledge that you have *perfect love* for yourself, your *perfect love* energy will assist your will power to reverse the programming that lets your addictive habit govern you. Be reminded again that *"Any good change that will come will come from the essence of your perfect love energy."* Become the master of your spirit, mind and body. You are now on your path to flourishing.

Addiction can be replaced with the "addiction" of living perfect love.

Self-Transformation to Stop Smoking

It is undisputed that smoking (and second-hand smoke) is dangerous to human health. Yet in spite of the broad publicity, this fact is continually given, millions of people continue to smoke. They are addicted. They manifest their need for oral pacification.

If you are a smoker, you probably have tried and failed to stop smoking in the past. Self-empowerment

Alpha rituals, because they reinforce your love for yourself and therefore your instinct to care for rather than harm your body, is a method that has worked successfully for the smokers I have treated.

Smoking — lighting your cigarette, taking the first puff, holding the cigarette between your fingers, puffing again, tapping ash from the tip, thinking, working, talking as you smoke — is a ritual in itself. If the cigarette were to appear in your mouth for you to take a puff, then disappear, then appear again, or be placed in your mouth for puffs by someone else, you would not take as much pleasure in the act of smoking at all. Experiment with this: Have someone else place a cigarette between your lips and hold it for you while you puff and inhale at regular intervals. You will probably find this awkward and far from the relaxing experience smoking has become for you. The point is that *smoking is a ritual you have created to calm you as it takes up time.* The hours of the day that stretch ahead of you are threatening and challenging, and your fearful perception of them is periodically lessened by the relaxing ritual of smoking. If you replace your smoking ritual with your Self-Empowerment Ritual several times a day, you are finding another way to reinforce your perception of the hours that loom ahead — one that lifts your spirits, relaxes you, and empowers you without harmful physical effects.

Oddly enough, most smokers find the habit of smoking distasteful in some way and yet they continue to smoke. Why not find another, positive ritual to replace this negative one? Your *perfect love* rituals will serve as just that.

The following questions will help you identify your smoking-related problem areas. As always, be truthful with your answers:

Your *perfect love* ritual will appease your oral needs.

142

1. Do you smoke more than you should?
2. Do you smoke immediately after meals or after sex?
3. Do you smoke when you are drinking alcohol?
4. Do you smoke while you watch TV?
5. Do you smoke when you are in an uncomfortable situation?
6. Do you smoke before breakfast?
7. Do you smoke more when you are around other smokers?
8. Do you wish you smoked less?
9. Has it been difficult for you to quit smoking?
10. Does it bother you when other people smoke?

Self-Empowerment Affirmations to Stop Smoking

Through the years, I have used many of these same affirmations with my clients. Nearly all the women I have counseled were able to achieve their self-improvement goals. Carefully contemplate these sample affirmations and select the ones you feel would help you achieve your *perfect love* self-empowerment goals.

1. I AM *perfect love* energy.
2. I AM the master of my spirit, mind and body.
3. I AM free from my need for oral pacification.
4. I AM free from the need to smoke.
5. I AM empowered to stop cigarette smoking.
6. I AM keeping my body healthy.
7. I AM free from my dependence on tobacco.
8. I AM replacing smoking with good habits.
9. I AM relaxed and calm without the need to smoke.
10. I AM free from the need to smoke when I am bored.
11. I AM able to get by daily without a cigarette.
12. I AM able to be in the company of others without the need to smoke.

Suggestion: *You may want to post your selected "I AM" affirmations on your bathroom mirror or some other place where you will see them regularly.*

Now, that you have completed reading the ten "I AM" affirmations, how do they make you feel? Take a moment and think about them.

Now ask yourself: Do I agree with them? Would I like them to be in my life?

Case History: Victoria's Victory Over Smoking

Victoria was 28 when she came to see me. She had started smoking at 15, and by then smoked two-and-a-half packs of cigarettes a day. Victoria realized she smoked excessively. She told me that she generally lit her first cigarette before breakfast and always when she was uncomfortable or bored. I suggested she try Alpha rituals and affirmations to try to break her long-term habit. Victoria agreed. In her mental-theater script, she saw herself smoking in the settings in which she typically "lit up" during the day — always at meals and usually around other people.

Victoria experiences her self-empowerment.

Using virtual-reality mental theater, she first practiced the ritual of self-love, then she re-created these scenes and imagined herself a non-smoker. She pictured herself offended by other people smoking cigarettes around her. She imagined herself putting a cigarette to her lips and finding it very distasteful. At strategic points during each day, Victoria took a break for an Alpha session rather than a cigarette. She found its effect calming and strengthening. To her joy, Victoria found herself lighting up fewer cigarettes as the weeks passed, and within a month or so was able to give up smoking altogether.

Self-Transformation for Overcoming Alcohol

Many people who have addictions such as smoking or drinking are not as keen to break their own addictions as the people who love them are to see them stop. If your motivation to stop an addictive habit is at someone else's prodding, *then it is not your desire at all.* You are not empowered to change your behavior and most likely your efforts will fail. *Memory, will, imagination and the physiology of your body all belong to you — and no one but you can undo the negative program inside you and build a positive program in its place.* I know that many of us wish there was some magic power or even someone or something that could force us to change. Just imagine if there was, we would become slaves to it and still be powerless. We should all be thankful that there is no such power or force outside of us that can control our appetites and desires. We must be a willing participant; only you have the power and authority to stop your addiction. Do not expect others to do it for you!

People all over the world get "high" or "buzzed" during times of celebration. While I stayed with the Rio Agua Clara natives, I was aware that their rituals satisfied their "high" At no time did I see abuse of any addictive substance or self-destructive behavior such as Westerners often display. My belief is that the natives were so grounded in their own self-worth and *perfect love* philosophy that it kept them spiritually, mentally and physically balanced. We in the Western world are so spiritually unbalanced that our bodies develop cravings for "feel-good" substances that we eventually cannot control. Addicts in our society are compelled to give up their substance altogether: In rare instances are they able to indulge "a little bit," for en-

The Agua Clara natives' ritual of *perfect love* kept them satisfied.

joyment only. It is either all or nothing — because the will on its own is often so weak.

The following questions will help you identify your alcohol-related problem areas. Be honest and truthful with your answers.

1. Do you drink alcohol to relax?
2. Do you drink alcohol until you are drunk?
3. Is it difficult for you to control how much alcohol you drink
4. Do you drink alcohol to forget feelings of guilt?
5. Do you drink when you are under pressure?
6. Do you drink when you are lonely or alone?
7. Do you think of yourself as a failure?
8. Do you feel unloved?
9. Does drinking make it easier for you to be with other people?
10. Have you tried to quit and failed?

After years of research and observation, I have concluded that most alcoholics, in spite of much blustering, loudness, and what seems like extroverted (outgoing) character, in fact possess very low self-esteem. They did not, however, begin this way. Their *perfect love* energy (which all of us are born with) was suppressed over the years until it became completely inactive and could no longer manifest itself. Eventually, inhibition takes over and they no longer feel comfortable around other people. Socializing often causes anxiety. So does work. A drink or several drinks allows them to relax. With alcohol, they are less conscious of their inhibitions; greatly relieved, they drink more and more. Once a drinker finds herself more comfortable when she drinks, alcohol becomes her constant companion and crutch. As chemical and cellular familiarity with alcohol grows in the body, the addiction becomes both physical and psychological. Now alcohol is the most important need in this person's life.

The secret to kicking an addiction rooted in low self-esteem and dislike of self is to program ourselves to love who we are, to accept ourselves perfectly. If we can do this, we have no need for inhibition and can be more outgoing. It is necessary to abstain from drinking alcohol while working with your affirmations and self-empowerment rituals. Your main objective should be building your self-confidence and self love: Use "I AM *perfect love* energy" and "I AM the master of my spirit, mind and body" as often as you can. With self-encouragement and self-love, you can break your addictive habit.

It is normal to want to feel good. Love yourself and others —it feels wonderful!

Case History: Dorothy Conquers Her Alcohol Addiction

Dorothy, 48, came to see me about her severe alcohol problem. She was alone and the mother of four children. She divorced her husband after she learned he was having affairs with other women. While they were together he did little to help her. He repeatedly put her down telling her she was worthless. She had been using alcohol since the age of 18, and she continued to drink more when she and her husband were fighting. She said she would drink because it made her feel better. She also needed to drink to feel more confident and sure of herself in the presence of others. Without alcohol, she felt tense and uncomfortable. Eventually she could not control her drinking and before she could realize, she had become addicted to alcohol. Feeling hopeless and powerless she came to me for help.

Together, we created a list of self-empowerment affirmations for Dorothy's low self-esteem and her reliance on alcohol to combat it. Practicing self-love regularly during her ritual sessions, Dorothy noticed that her entire feeling toward herself and others was changing. Six months into the sessions, Dorothy realized she had been getting along quite comfortably without alcohol in her life. Because of her commitment to self-love and because she truly believes in her own worth, Dorothy is able to enjoy life free of alcohol. The foundation is her *perfect love* energy for all that occurs in her world. Dorothy is strong; she has found harmony and no longer needs or wants to destroy herself.

Affirmations for Conquering Alcohol

Through the years, I have used many of these same "I AM" affirmations with my clients. Nearly all the women I have counseled were able to achieve their self-improvement goals. Carefully look over these sample affirmations and select the ones you feel would help you achieve your *perfect love* self-empowerment goals.

1. I AM *perfect love* energy.
2. I AM the master of my spirit, mind and body.
3. I AM no longer controlled by alcohol.
4. I AM no longer finding it necessary to drink for any reason whatsoever.
5. I AM the most important person to me.
6. I AM a self-empowered woman who does not need alcohol to make me feel good.
7. I AM increasing my self-confidence each day without the use of alcohol.
8. I AM able to enjoy people without having to drink alcohol.
9. I AM loving myself and my new alcohol-free image.
10. I AM an intelligent woman: I make decisions to protect my health and happiness and the health and happiness of others.

Suggestion: *You may want to post your selected "I AM" affirmations on your bathroom mirror or some other place where you will see them regularly.*

Now, that you have completed reading the ten "I AM" affirmations, think about how you are feeling about some of them? Take a moment and contemplate — ask yourself: How do they make me feel? Do I want to change any of them? Do I want to really experience them in my life?

"I AM"

Daily
in Every Way
Getting Better
and Better

CHAPTER

Self-Empowerment Rituals for Conquering Pain

This chapter is included for women wishing to apply their Self-Empowerment Ritual effectively to relieve and control organic and psychosomatic pain. Clients who have come to me with arthritis, back and neck pain, headaches and chronically aching muscles have used the Self-Empowerment Alpha Ritual with great success. Any or all of the following pain-management methods may help you relieve your pain. Psychosomatic or functional pain generally responds better to relaxation methods of management. If you are experiencing severe organic pain, you may experiment with any of pain-control techniques in this chapter. *The author of this book recommends that you consult your physician regarding any of the pain management ritual exercises in this book before beginning.* Whether your pain is functional or organic, you can learn to regulate your response to pain signals. In this way you learn to manage pain.

It is helpful to remove your fears, before you try to eliminate pain.

151

Most people who suffer from pain are compelled to resort to drugs for relief. Both opiates and analgesics alleviate pain by slowing down the central nervous system, thereby blocking the message carrying current from signaling the brain. A person on these medications does not feel pain because of this drugging effect. Drugs do not act on a specific pain-causing area. They deaden the entire body including the brain. If you have ever taken an opiate or an analgesic, you may recall its effect on your physical and mental reactions. The most common pain reliever, aspirin, affects our body in much the same way as the stronger medications. Extensive research has documented the detrimental effects of continued use of any drug for pain relief. One of the dangers of using these drugs is that it eventually leads to addiction. If you are already addicted to prescription drugs, Chapter 9, The Power of *Perfect Love* to Conquer Addiction, can be very helpful.

Remember, whenever you want something too much, it will soon make you powerless!

The Self-Empowerment Ritual session may be applied to the management of pain. In following this natural, living *perfect love* method, you utilize your self-empowerment resources of self-regulation. Before you begin to practice a Self-Empowerment Alpha Ritual to control body pain, it must be understood that in most instances, severe pain serves as an alarm for some injury or malfunction within the body. *You should never attempt to eliminate pain until you understand the cause for that pain signal.* Without such a warning system, we would be unable to protect ourselves from injury or illness. Persons suffering with prolonged pain should first consult a physician before undertaking any self-help therapy. Pain can be divided into two categories — *organic (physical)* and psychosomatic (*psychological or functional*). You feel organic pain when injury or disease damages the cells and tissues in your body. When your pain has no apparent physical origin, meaning it does not stem from injury or disease damage, it is psychosomatic in origin, or triggered by your mental thoughts.

Both organic and functional pain will become more severe and prolonged when aggravated by anxiety and tension. Deep relaxation will usually lessen pain noticeably. Relaxation for pain control is used by physicians and dentists. You may recall your dentist's instructions to relax, or if you have experienced a serious injury you probably remember the physician's directions that you lie still, rest and relax.

Relaxation helps you overcome shock and anxiety and in this way helps relieve body tension. Some areas of pain control in which Self-Empowerment Alpha rituals are helpful are muscular-skeletal disorders, arthritis, backache headaches and neck pains. Many of these pains are frequently functional in origin. People experiencing functional pain will find they are able to control the pain and usually relieve it entirely with continued Self-Empowerment Alpha Rituals.

"Alpha 25" is your key to deep relaxation.

Energy of Love Conquers Pain

The idea behind all pain management is creating a sense of security and comfort. Feelings of insecurity, fear, discomfort, irritation, anger and powerlessness will all aggravate your pain and generally worsen most aspects of your life. While most pain is real and by no means imaginary, there is much we *can do with our imagination* to turn it into something less threatening, less controlling, and less capable of making us unhappy.

153

Living perfect love teaches us to create an "energy of love" between ourselves and our pain. When your mental concept of your energy of love is strong enough, you will be able to feel its softness and its comfort *more than you feel your pain.* The energy of love is real when you believe in it. You owe it to yourself to make your own life better, and its energy comes from the well of self-love and self-caring within you. If you look around, you will see that others offer you their energy of love as well — *when you let them.* Make use of this aid. Learn to recognize and appreciate it, and most of all, learn that you, yourself, can create it.

The Self-Empowerment Alpha Ritual works effectively to relieve and control organic and psychosomatic pain. Clients who have come to me with arthritis, back and neck pain, headaches and chronically aching muscles have used *Living Perfect Love* exercises with great success. Any or all of the following pain-management methods may help you relieve your pain. The first is a basic relaxation ritual that does not affect your brain wave level; the exercises that follow require that you enter a state of Alpha before you continue to proceed. Remember that psychosomatic or functional pain generally responds better to relaxation methods of management. If you are experiencing severe organic pain, you may experiment with any of pain-control techniques in this chapter.

Let go of your conscious awareness of time and you will let go of the pain.

Basic Relaxation Ritual

Please assume a comfortable position, either sitting or reclining. Concentrate on relaxing your body completely. Begin with your feet and legs, then think about your hands. Continue until you have thought about letting every part of your body become loose. Allow

154

your body to go limp. Avoid thinking about the area in which you feel pain. Notice only the feeling of relaxation as it spreads through your body.

Pay attention to the blood flowing through your body and concentrate on feeling this circulation slowing down as you relax more and more.

Concentrate on your breathing and feel it slowing down slightly. Take a deep breath, hold it to the count of five and then exhale completely, feeling all of the air leave your body. Repeat this breathing exercise three times.

Focus on the thought of your body settling down. You are completely at rest and you are feeling relaxation throughout your entire body. You no longer think about any sensation of pain, but rather you enjoy the tranquil feeling of total relaxation.

Five methods for management of pain are discussed in the following pages. Detailed instructions are given for temperature increase, loving glove numbing method, paradox for pain control, distraction for pain control and detachment or denial for pain control.

Your Mental Heating Pad Ritual

This method of pain management should be used only in relieving pain from muscular and skeletal problems. Following the Self-Empowerment Alpha Ritual, practice your virtual reality mental theater.

It is the *perfect love* energy of the sun that warms and heals us.

This is a virtual realistic experience. You vividly imagine experiencing an increase of temperature in the area of your body in which you feel discomfort.

Symptom Feedback Method for Temperature Control

As you already know, it takes several minutes to achieve temperature change. You must be patient and take your time, as you have already done in previous Self-Empowerment Alpha Ritual sessions.

Concentrate on warmth in the area you feel pain sensation. Vividly imagine you have a heating pad or hot water bottle resting over the place you feel discomfort. You are able to increase that temperature gradually by using your imagination. As you know, in all vivid imaginary exercise you must generate the feelings of the experience you are imagining. Feel the warmth from the heat source. You may aid the temperature increase by making direct contact with the pain area. If possible, place your hand over the area where you are experiencing discomfort.

As you feel the temperature of the spot increasing, you begin to feel better and better. You are master of your mind and body. Your energy of love creates a warm softness right over the spot on your hand. Your energy of love is taking care of you. You are a self-empowered woman whose mind and body, through love, can diminish and eliminate pain.

The Loving Glove Numbing Method

An individual can learn control over both organic and functional pain. The loving glove numbing method for management of pain is especially useful because it is a most effective way of transferring numbness from one part of the body to another. Often with acute pain it is difficult to control the particular area of discomfort; it is easier to decrease sensation in a neutral part of your body and then transfer the numbness to the pain area.

It is good for you to recall the insulating feeling of wearing gloves.

As in other pain management methods, you follow the Self-Empowerment Alpha Ritual, using the virtual reality mental theater technique combined with the help of some else giving you the suggestions. As you practice the loving glove numbing you will experience a sensation of numbness, it is similar to having a thick soft glove over your hand. After you have completely numbed your hand, it will feel as if it had fallen asleep.

While at *"Alpha level 25,"* vividly imagine a mental theater scene in which you dip the hand you choose to numb into a bucket of ice water. With your hand in the icy water. Your skin begins to tingle with the sensation of cold.

Never say, "My pain." It is not your pain. Don't own it.

Next imagine your other hand in a bucket of warm water. Vividly picture the two buckets with your hands in each of them. Feel the warmth of the water on your hand. Think about the contrast between the two buckets of water; feel the difference in each hand. As you have learned with the vivid imaginary exercises, you must make your mental theater exercise very realistic. In order to achieve control you must actually experience the sensations of hot and cold. In a short while, the hand you have in the ice water bucket will begin to feel numb, just as if you had placed your hand into freezing water. It is not necessary to experience total numbness, but you will have a sense of decreased circulation and tingling. Most sensation will be gone.

Contrast Method

If you have trouble using either temperature control or loving glove numbness, you might begin your Self-Empowerment Ritual for pain management with the contrast method. Often we will cooperate with releas-

I saw my friend Omar remove pain from his burned hand by adding more heat it.

157

ing pain sensation when we are first convinced that we have the control to increase discomfort. The contrast method is an indirect approach to pain control.

With the contrast method you begin by increasing the pain experience. This is accomplished as you practice virtual reality mental theater. As you realistically imagine yourself relaxing completely, your programming affirmations are directing you to increase the sensations of pain. As you do this, you raise your pain threshold. Insert the following verbal script in your ritual.

Contrast Program Affirmations

"Just as I am capable of increasing pain in my body, I also am equally capable of decreasing this same pain." At the count of five my feeling of pain will have increased noticeably. 1 ... 2 ... 3 ... I concentrate on the feeling of pain ... 4 ... 5. Feeling this increased pain, I realize I have the ability to control the degree to pain. I have the self control to relieve my body pain, just as I have been able to increase that same pain.

Counting from five back down to one, I will reduce the pain sensation. With each reducing number the pain will lessen more and more. When I reach the number one, the pain will feel as it did before I began counting. 5 ... 4 ... 3 ... the pain is lessening with each reducing number ... 2 ... 1. Continuing to count, with each reducing number the pain will continue to lessen. Minus 1 ... minus 2 ... I feel the pain decreasing more and more. As I count I feel less and less body sensation ... minus 3 ... minus 4 ... my body is becoming numb and insensitive, the pain I previously felt is disappearing.

Take your time. There is no hurry. Move at a comfortable rate.

Where I felt pain, I now feel numbness ... minus 5 ... minus 6 ... my body feels cool and relaxed ... minus 7 ... minus 8 ... I feel no discomfort or pain anywhere in my body ... minus 9 ... minus 10. As I hear the number minus 10, I am completely relaxed and free from pain." If you continue to experience any pain, continue counting yourself down until you are in a state of total relaxation.

Distraction Method

The distraction method of pain control is easily learned. You simply draw your attention from the area of discomfort by concentrating on another part of your body, or an object in your environment. For example, you had suffered an injury to your right foot, you would be able to lessen that pain by concentrating on your right hand. Your degree of distraction will be more complete if you focus on something of particular interest to you. If the pain is severe, concentrate on things which are very important to you. You might entertain the vivid thought of being with someone you love; as you have learned with vivid visualization, you can actually feel that you are with that person. As you do this, you draw your attention away from your pain.

By entering *"Alpha 25,"* you naturally experience distraction.

The distraction method is most effective when it is necessary to accomplish immediate alleviation of pain. It is not imperative that you be in the Alpha brain wave state in order to have success with distraction. It is a useful pain control method for any emergency situation.

Detachment and Denial Methods

In both the detachment and denial methods of pain management you learn to regard the pain sensation as an experience apart from your body. Pain only exists because you acknowledge the sensation. Detachment and denial rituals teach us to control this pain message. If you are able to enter *"Alpha level 25"* and can sustain this level without distraction or interruption, you can prevent your mind from registering pain.

Detachment Method

While relaxing at *"Alpha level 25,"* use the virtual reality mental theater technique and realistically imagine seeing yourself. As you do so, you clearly acknowledge the area in which you are feeling pain. Focus on the pain area and interpret that pain sensation as a piece of clothing which you are wearing. Tell yourself that just as you are able to remove that garment from your body, as you would any clothing, in the very same manner you are able to remove the pain. Create a detailed mental theater experience, as you have already learned. As you remove the clothing, you feel the pain leaving your body. If you do not shed the discomfort the first time you imagine removing the clothing, repeat the exercise until you are successful.

You are now empowered to remove the pain infected clothing from your body.

It is essential that you have a very realistic picture of the pain sensation as a tangible garment. With concentration this becomes very acceptable and real. Your vivid imaginary control must be excellent in order for you to actually feel the detachment of pain as you shed the clothing.

160

Denial Method

As with the detachment exercise of pain control, the denial method depends on a very vivid imagination as well as the capacity for excellent vivid imaginary experience. While relaxing at *"Alpha level 25,"* you use the virtual reality mental theater technique. Realistically picture a large switch directly in front of you. The switch is within your reach. From the switch you follow a line to an electric fan. You see the fan turning rapidly. As the fan turns you continue to feel pain. The rotation of the fan is identified with your sensation of pain. As long as the fan continues to turn, you will feel pain.

You have control of the switch. When you turn the switch you will stop the fan. Realistically imagine lifting your arm and turning the switch. As you do so, look at the fan; you see it is beginning to slow down. While you watch the fan gradually slowing, you feel your pain sensation also diminishing. Focus on the fan blades as they continue to slow down, and your pain also lessens more and more. When the fan comes to a complete stop, your pain will also be gone.

You are the power that turns the switch. *Turn the switch now!*

Remember, your feeling of pain was identified with the movement of the fan; when the fan stops, you no longer feel any pain. You deny all sensation of discomfort. Repeat this exercise as long as your pain persists, you must continue to practice the denial method. With practice you will learn to closely identify your pain with the picture of the moving fan. When you tell yourself your pain is decreasing as the fan slows down, you will find that in fact you are becoming free from the pain experience. As with all Self-Empowerment Ritual sessions your skill with your ritual increases as you practice the training progression.

Afterword

It is my hope that *Living Perfect Love, Self-Empowerment Rituals for Women* will serve as a guide for women in their endeavor for self-empowerment. The benefits of Living Perfect Love are many; each woman finds the personal application for the self empowerment Alpha rituals. This book is intended to be an informative summary and workbook to teach you Self-Empowerment Alpha rituals.

Part One has made you aware of the ancient wisdom as practiced by the Rio Agua Clara natives in the Colombian jungles. In this revised text of *Alphagenics* I have attempted to embrace the many wise teaching of the Rio Agua Clara natives. Most important, we learn *"any good change that will come will come from the essence of our perfect love energy."*

Both primitive philosophy and Western "New Age" teaching are fundamental to living *perfect love*. The primitive Colombian natives and the New Age thought bring to us the time-tested methods of meditation and self-empowerment.

Part Two discusses the valuable ability which we all share — the innate potential for self-empowerment of our spirits, our minds and our bodies. No one can give you the art of self-empowerment; you alone possess the possibility for your personal fulfillment and happiness. It is my role to act as a guide and reveal to you your natural energies and skills. The more carefully you study this text, the more completely you will master self-empowerment of spirit, mind and body. Always be mindful that the expansive ability for self-healing and continued health and happiness rests within each of us.

Part Three presents the dynamics of living *perfect love* Self-Empowerment Alpha Ritual programming for women. The many details of the exercises have been illustrated for you. While you are not expected to read all of the programming areas, you will probably find one or two programs which are of interest to you. Carefully follow the discussion of any single programming area and you should have no trouble designing your own living *perfect love* program.

All three parts of the *Living Perfect Love, Self-Empowerment Rituals for Women* are essential to your understanding and practice of the empowerment rituals. You are the key in making the Self-Empowerment Alpha rituals a reality in your life. The self-empowerment programming will be effective only with your determined effort. Remember, it has taken you considerable time to acquire any problem you may have; allow yourself time to overcome this difficulty. Be patient and realize that many women have achieved success with living *perfect love*.

Finally, it is my most sincere wish that you completely embrace Ag'nike's truth of living *perfect love* convincingly knowing that you, above all, *love yourself* and allow that self-love to exhibit your self-empowerment.

Above all, love yourself.

You have now learned how to receive the love, respect, affection, abundance and perfect health you deserve.

Index

INDEX

INDEX

INDEX

INDEX

INDEX

INDEX

Biography

Dr. Angelo Zaffuto received his doctorate in sociology from St. Andrews Episcopal University in London, England in 1967. Dr. Zaffuto has spent a lifetime researching the effects of negative programming on people's and especially women's lives. Today he teaches Ag'nike's Alpha Waterfall Rituals, caring for clients with problems of low self-esteem, anxiety, overweight and addiction. He teaches self-empowerment courses for women: *Increasing Self-Esteem and Self-Worth*.

Dr. Zaffuto has spent many years counseling and guiding people in trouble. His focus and efforts resulted in the renowned Santa Barbara (California) Alphagenic Center, where he introduced the method of self-improvement known as *Alphagenics*. Dr. Zaffuto published *Alphagenics: How to Use Your Brain Waves to Improve Your Life* in 1974 (Doubleday New York N.Y.).

He is president of the Humantics Foundation for Women a non profit California Corporation which he founded in 1963, with the purpose of supporting women of all ages to reclaim their birthright — personal power — while embodying their feminine spirit and deepest truths.

Always an adventurer, Dr. Zaffuto traveled in 1980 to South America to dredge for gold. The "gold" he found was the ancient wisdom of a small native tribe on the banks of the Rio Agua Clara, deep in the Colombian jungle. Led by Ag'nike, a Medicine Woman, Dr. Zaffuto witnessed rituals for mental and physical healing that have changed his consciousness. He shares them with us in this revised book, *Living Perfect Love: Self-Empowerment Rituals for Women*.

BOOK & TAPE ORDER FORM

Ag'nike's Waterfall Ritual: audio cassette tape - 60 minutes
Dr. Angelo Zaffuto and Anita Coolidge guide the listener in a real life-like
experience of Ag'nike's Self-Empowerment *WATERFALL RITUAL.*

☐ LPL-2-X   Ag'nike's Ritual Tape, ~~Reg. $12.95~~, (limited time) __ __ $ 6.50 ea.
☐ LPL-4-6   Self-Empowerment "I AM" Affirmation Cards __ __ __ __ $ 9.95 set
☐ LPL-0-3   *Living Perfect Love* (book) __ __ __ __ __ __ __ __ __ __ $11.95 ea.
☐ HFW-3-8   *Breast Implants*:
            The Myths, The Facts, The Women (donation)__ __ __ __ $ 9.95 ea.
☐ Please send me information — speakers and workshops.

ADD: shipping and handling cost for each item: __ __ __ __ __ __ $ 3.50
CA residents add sales tax: 8.5%
Call or write for special discount price for quantity orders.

Most of these items can be ordered from your local book store,
or you can use the following Order Form. Thank you.

Name: _____

Address: _____ Unit.# _____

City: _____ State: _____

Credit Card: MC/Visa/Discovery/AmEx: _____ Personal Check: _____

Credit Card #: _____ _____ _____ Exp. Date: _____

Signature: _____ Date: _____

Send to: Pandora's Products
6965 El Camino Real #105-105
Rancho La Costa, CA 92009
Allow delivery time of 3 - 4 weeks. Personal checks are 5 - 7 weeks.

The Humantics Foundation for Women
The Humantics Foundation for Women exists to help and support women of all ages to reclaim
their birthright—personal power—while embodying their feminine spirit and truths. The Humantics
Foundation is a not-for-profit 501,(C)(3) California Corporation. For information, write to Ilena
Rosenthal, Foundation Director and author of *Breast Implants: The Myth, The Facts, The Women,
A Comprehensive Research Document with Substantiated Evidence of the Harmful Conse-
quences of Breast Implants.* You can obtain copies, by using the above order form and paying by
credit card, or by sending a check for $9.95 to the Humantics Foundation for Women (tax de-
ductible. Fed. ID #95-2664938):

Ilena Rosenthal
Humantics Foundation for Women
1380 Garnet Ave. Suite 444
San Diego, CA 92109
e-mail: ilena@connectnet.com